SEVEN SECULAR CHALLENGES *Facing* 21st-CENTURY CATHOLICS

Val J. Peter

PAULIST PRESS
New York/Mahwah, NJ

Cover and book design by Lynn Else

Library of Congress Cataloging-in-Publication Data

Peter, Val J.
  Seven secular challenges facing 21st-century Catholics / Val J. Peter.
    p. cm.
  Includes bibliographical references.
  ISBN 978-0-8091-4570-6 (alk. paper)
  1. Catholic Church—History—21st century. 2. Christianity and culture.
I. Title.
  BX1390.P48 2009
  282.09′051—dc22

                                                              2008019799

Published by Paulist Press
997 Macarthur Boulevard
Mahwah, New Jersey 07430

www.paulistpress.com

Printed and bound in the
United States of America

CONTENTS

INTRODUCTION

This is an upbeat book about a very important topic. Many of us enjoy the hustle and bustle of postmodern life: the medical advances that help us stay healthy, the communications revolution that includes the Internet, ubiquitous cell phones, the iPod, and so much more. Terrific movies, videos, and DVDs abound. Many believe that the immigrants moving to America will enrich us all if we are open to it.

The post-Vatican II liturgical reforms such as celebrating the Mass in the vernacular, the opportunity to receive holy communion in the hand and from the cup, the use of lay ministers in the life of the church exemplify the spiritual renewal that many of us enjoy and appreciate. We are grateful for these changes and advances that affect our lives in a positive way.

However, at the same time one may be uncritical and unaware of some harmful elements of the postmodern culture, elements that may pose a threat to our spiritual lives. This book is an attempt to identify some of these troublesome elements that challenge us as well as to suggest some successful strategies to employ for ourselves and our families. Every culture has glaring flaws and today is no exception.

This book points to seven critical areas and challenges where our culture is not enriching, but rather diminishing our lives, precisely at a time when men and women desperately feel the need for spiritual strength and moral courage. These may be called seven secular challenges. This book suggests successful strategies for dealing with them in our lives. Some of these may be described as the "idols of our times."

What are these secular challenges? What are some successful strategies available to overcome them?

The first major challenge is **diminished respect for authority,** that is, civil authority, parental authority, the authority of the gospels, and the authority of the church. Why is authority in trouble? There are both secular reasons and religious reasons for this. The most successful strategy is to develop a new, uniquely postmodern respect for authority. It entails not necessarily developing the kind of respect of the past, but a respect that resonates thoroughly in the very being of us all. (Chapters 1–3)

The second secular challenge is **uncritical openness,** the widespread belief that one is free to experience everything. Contemporary society seems to embrace an openness that is very uncritical. The most successful strategy will entail selective, critical openness. How is it developed? (Chapter 4)

The third secular challenge is **cynicism.** In these postmodern times one seems to breathe a cynical air. About what are we most cynical? Not just politicians or clergy, for there is cynicism about families and even about life itself. There is too much cynicism about religion, even though there are things we should be cynical about. This is counterproductive to spirituality. There are effective ways to say no to cynicism. One needs to learn them and practice them. (Chapter 5)

The fourth secular challenge is **the embracing of ideology**. The opposite of ideology is idealism. Ideology sees the world through a dark lens with a single, narrow focus. The remedy for mistaken ideological beliefs is not to give up believing but to develop better control over these beliefs. The vast majority of Catholics are not ideologues in any sense of the term. They see light and darkness, not viewing the world solely through a small dark lens. They do not become obsessive and are not controlled by hatred and anger. But many are overly influenced by ideologues in our church and society. This has a negative effect on how the individual lives one's life. (Chapter 6)

The fifth secular challenge is **learned helplessness,** and the remedy for it is self-efficacy. There are ways to neutralize it so that our spiritual lives may not be impaired. (Chapter 7)

Anti-intellectualism is the sixth secular challenge, and the successful strategy to overcome it is to discover anew the importance of learning in a postmodern world. Anti-intellectualism seems to have always been a strong current in America. But with a media-dominated postmodern society, intellectual flabbiness brings subtle new perils to our spirituality. Here, too, there are antidotes that can render the poison harmless. (Chapter 8)

The seventh secular challenge is **political correctness.** In our time, this involves the supersophisticated marketing tools of social manipulation that suddenly change people's views without their even knowing what is happening. This is environmental conditioning, an instrument to gain power, and has nothing to do with the truth. If political correctness begins to prevail in a person's life, the message of the gospel is in danger of becoming a thin veneer and nothing more. (Chapter 9)

This book attempts to present strategies that will help you succeed in all these areas. These strategies will provide exceptional support for your spiritual life in our own times. And the more you think of these relevant topics, the more you may see this as the way to rejuvenate your spirit and your life.

I have been working with "throwaway children" for more than two decades. At the beginning, it was not clear to me how toxic these elements of our culture were, elements that were sweeping our young people out to sea on a tide of despair and alienation. Then it dawned on me these elements are noxious, not only for my boys and girls, but also for all of us. Every culture and society have positive and negative elements. Ours is no exception. These negative elements impact our church in America and all of us. These seven strategies will bridge the gaps in your life and make everything connect for you.

The church is always in need of reform. That applies to me, you, all of us. Always? Yes, always. And sometimes the need for purification, for integration, is more urgent than at other times. This book promotes key categories of spiritual growth, catechesis training, and scripture study. Those who have gone before us have said powerful, inspiring things about the need for reform in our lives and in the church. Let us listen to them and learn how they faced the challenges of their times.

In the fifth century, St. Augustine teaches: "Wherever in these books I have mentioned the Church not having spot or wrinkle, should not be interpreted as if it were such now, but rather what it is being prepared to be when, indeed, it will appear glorious. For now, because of certain ignorance and infirmities of its members, its condition is such that every day the Church says: Forgive us our trespasses."[1]

In the sixth century, Gregory the Great points out: "St. Paul says: 'If a man desires the office of a bishop he desires a good work.' We must observe that St. Paul said this at a time when whoever was set over the people was first to be led to the tortures of martyrdom. So, indeed, it was praiseworthy to seek the episcopate when, in consequence of holding the office, there was no doubt that its hold would meet with the most severe sufferings. But it behooves a bishop to be blameless…he (St. Paul) therefore approves the desire but warns these people by his precept as though he plainly said: 'I praise what you seek, but acquaint yourselves first with what you are seeking, lest…you become the most blameworthy and detestable in that you hasten to be seen by all on the pinnacle of honor.'"[2]

The same St. Gregory does not hesitate to say: "No one does more harm in the Church than he who, having the title or rank of holiness, acts evilly."[3]

In the thirteenth century, St. Thomas Aquinas says: "That the Church may be glorious, without spot or wrinkle, is the final goal to which we are being led through the passion of Christ. It will be so only in our eternal home, not on our journey there, during which, if we said we had no sin we should be deceiving ourselves, as we are told in the First Epistle of St. John."[4]

In the twentieth century, Hans Urs von Balthasar writes: "The New Testament never talks about the assurances given to the church of Christ without mentioning in the same breath the threat of abuse, the possibility of defection. Nowhere is the spotlessness of the bride a fait accompli which the bride need only to accept and worry about no longer. Precisely the relevant saying of Paul shows this quite clearly: I feel a divine jealousy for you, for I betrothed you to Christ to present you as a pure bride to her one husband. But I am afraid that as the serpent deceived Eve by his cunning, your thoughts will be led astray from a sincere and pure devotion to Christ."[5]

So let us begin.

Chapter 1

SECULAR REASONS
FOR WHY AUTHORITY
IS IN TROUBLE

If today there are any secular challenges at all, disrespect for authority, especially the authority of God, has to be at the very top of the list.

This chapter will point out some very powerful, subtle secular reasons why authority is in trouble and will stimulate our minds and hearts to figure out what to do in response.

This world of ours seems to have frequently dimmed the light of authority, impugned its rightful role, and mocked its helpfulness in our lives. Many people reading this will say, "Yes, that's true and it's what authority deserves." This antiauthoritarian sentiment first hit me square between the eyes in the alienated adolescents coming to Boys Town decades ago. They were angry and oppositional/ defiant. *"No one's going to tell me what to do."* This is "in-your-face anger." It tends to be reinforced over and over again by the mainstream of popular, secular American culture: music, films, videos, television, and radio. Over time it became clear not just how widespread it was, but how reinforced this antiauthoritarian view was not only among adolescents, but across

1

the general population. My Boys Town youth were simply an exaggerated artifact of a huge throng.

What happened to customary respect for authority, which up until recent times was the wisdom of the ages? What happened to the notion that even if you engage in independent thinking, normally you express it in terms respectful of authority? Why is it much easier to ridicule authority today? What happened to create such mistrust?

HISTORICAL REASONS

Part of the answer can be found in the abuse of power in recent history, starting in the twentieth century with figures such as Joseph Stalin and Adolf Hitler, followed by Chairman Mao, Pol Pot, and Idi Amin, all claiming legitimate authority while abusing it. The civil rights movement of the 1960s is memorialized by "We Shall Overcome." Whom shall we overcome? Legitimate civil authority abusing its power by enforcing ugly segregation. In the Vietnam War, our children's pride in and affection for their country were shattered with the battering ram of "Hey, hey, LBJ, how many boys have you killed today?" Then Richard Nixon was forced to resign due to his abuse of authority in Watergate. Pope Paul VI's efforts to stamp out dissent with the 1968 *Humanae vitae* produced charges and countercharges in the media that churchmen were abusing authority. Ecology and feminism made their contribution in their attacks on a so-called male-dominated society. All of these historical events helped create an antiauthoritarian culture in which issuing more commands did little good and calls for moderation found little support.

This horrendous abuse of authority on such a broad scale produced shock waves through the healing professions and the media in our beloved country. After World War II (Hitler), and during the cold war (Stalin), a series of clever elitist authors, scholars, and child-care experts conditioned by the violence and totalitarian control of the World War II era gained media attention, selling the idea that the traditional age-old honorable child rearing and educational practices were violence prone, overly authoritarian, and thus to be rejected as unhealthy and harmful. This was a frontal assault on parental authority.

SOCIETAL CONSIDERATIONS

It is hard to overestimate the impact this had on our culture. It was an attack on the bedrock of civilization, namely, the family itself. Consider some examples.[1]

Many are familiar with Dr. Benjamin Spock, who taught new mothers not only about diaper rash, but, in addition, gained national attention by chastising the traditional approach of parents to raising their children.[2] He called it authoritarian, heavy-handed, unfair, and unproductive. Punishment, said Spock, is not healthy for child and mother. Punitive disciplinary practices need to be abandoned. In his introduction to *Baby and Child Care* (1945), he spoke of the threat of nuclear war as motivating his writings. He saw the horrific examples of misuse of authority in wartime Germany and Japan and concluded that it was authority that was to blame rather than its misuse. Punishment became a culprit. His authority was enormous. In 1967 he abandoned the practice of medicine to join the antiwar movement. He ran for president in 1972 on the People's Party ticket. His thesis: If nations need to disarm, so do parents and other authority figures.

This was the beginning of a flood of antiauthoritarian books. Haim Ginott, *Between Parent and Child* (1965)[3] and *Between Parent and Teenager* (1969),[4] took up the attack on traditional parenting. So did Thomas Gordon in *P.E.T. Parent Effectiveness Training* (1970).[5]

Traditionally, parents knew that, if they were to develop a conscience in their offspring, they had to lay down the law about lying, cheating, and stealing. They had to back up their words with real authority. Ginott, Gordon, and so many others began to say this was all wrong. Parents should be therapists, not moralists. They should use a counseling approach, not an authoritarian style. This approach became widely praised and enormously popular and helped create a generation of out-of-control teenagers, especially amid the middle and upper-middle class. The psychoanalyst Rudolf Dreikurs, in *The Challenge of Parenthood* (1958), told parents to embrace democracy by having family councils.[6] Some parents even gave their children voting rights. It all seemed so good, but the results were not very positive.

Bishops and pastors were encouraged to abandon sternness and adopt a pastoral approach, which too often was interpreted in America as something like positive parenting. Vatican II and pop culture got all mixed up. After all, Vatican II's *Church in the Modern World* (1965) strongly recommended being open to new advances in research and science. Unfortunately, numerous theologians, religious educators, priests, and bishops accepted naively and uncritically this wave of psychoanalytic thinking and humanistic psychology flooding larger society without taking into consideration the very serious deficiencies and even fatal flaws contained therein. Stovepiping with a silo effect was common. (For those unfamiliar with the terms *stovepiping* and *silo effect*, see my definition on page 28.) This is not a call to reject the psychological sciences, but it is a call to adopt a critical, integrated approach.

By the 1980s, the problems of drugs, alcohol, sexual promiscuity, and defiance of authority so made their mark among adolescents that a new wave of experts took to the media advising a midcourse correction. These gurus said there must be at least *some* parental authority, *some* negative consequences for inappropriate (avoid the word *immoral*) behavior, but nothing physical, nothing violent. Everything therapeutic. The midcourse correction was mild and ineffective. Dana Mack in her *The Assault on Parenthood* (1997)[7] uses Lee and Marlene Cantor's 1985 work, *Assertive Discipline for Parents* as an example:

> Many parents have been told by contemporary child-rearing experts that for the well being of their children, no matter how badly they behave, the parents should avoid "stern" or "authoritarian" approaches and find alternative psychological approaches. These include talking to their children about why they misbehaved (counseling approach), negotiating with their children to change the problem behavior (democratic approach), and/or praising their children only when they behave (behavior modification approach). Each of these approaches has merit; however, none of them provides you with an answer for what to do when you use them and your child still will not behave.[8]

Emergence of a Self-Centered Culture

However, it was too little and too late. The culture of child raising was thoroughly antiauthoritarian. We were raising children who were selfish in the extreme. Ours became a self-centered culture that could be described as a culture of "I deserve" and "I come first." It became a culture that teaches us to feel good about saying, "I will help others only to the degree that it helps me." These youngsters grew up and became parents.

The first work of Alice Miller, a Swiss psychoanalyst, *For Your Own Good: Hidden Cruelty in Child-Rearing and the Roots of Violence* (1983),[9] then arrived on the shores of America with an ominous message. Overreacting to World War II, especially how young Germans raised by authoritarian parents willingly followed Hitler's orders, she taught parents that in their childhood they were themselves victims. So if these stern parents were unsuccessful in raising their children the reason was simple. They themselves were "unwitting slaves to the dark secrets of their own childhood."

She used Hitler as an example of a person who was a victim of his own childhood, rather than the immoral monster that he was perceived to be. Her conclusion? "Nothing is ever gained by assigning guilt." In other words, the implication is that it was not Hitler's fault. If it was not Hitler's fault, then it was not my fault or your fault that we failed as parents. This kind of thinking had a profound impact on the elite in America. In her next book, *Drama of the Gifted Child* (1984), Miller accused parents of the crime of inculcating traditional Judeo-Christian values in their offspring.[10] The feminist movement and media movers or shakers in the media had a field day with this.

PBS aired a ten-week series on the family produced by a New Age prophet, John Bradshaw. Out with sin and guilt; in with positive praise.[11] Bradshaw says authoritarian parents are guilty of "soul murder" and even responsible for the My Lai massacre.

Not surprisingly then, by 1981, the famous pollster, Daniel Yankelovich *(New Rules)*, began to report a huge shift in how Americans look at life, a shift away from strict subordination of self to external goals and toward internal goals of self-fulfillment.[12] Such a strategy renders external authority superfluous. What are these inner goals: How can I grow, how can I utilize my potential, how can I find self-fulfillment, how can I realize the duty I have to myself? The idea is this: The more inner needs fulfilled, the greater the self-fulfillment.

Other Influences

All of this is manifestly at odds with the gospel message of Christian self-denial, but this view triumphed. It is clearly false to say that the more of my needs that are fulfilled, the greater is my self-fulfillment. Why? Because our needs include so many self-contradictory desires that we have to neglect some of them if we are to avoid becoming a mass of contradictions.

What Yankelovich described as the ethic of self-fulfillment was the result of the widespread acceptance of these elements of popularized humanistic psychology and positive parenting. It was not that this form of psychology had nothing good to say. It had much good to say, but the things it said that were not good were also praised and copied.

In a brief overview of other influences, let us begin with Carl Rogers, who was one of the great founders of a new movement. His impact upon the clerical culture in America was enormous. He began what we call today the human potential movement. In 1948, a report circulated regarding the Cambridge Summerville Delinquency Project, showing that Rogers's nondirective counseling helped delinquent boys to be less likely to get in trouble again with the law. He became well known.

By 1960, he published *On Becoming a Person*, popularizing the idea that, to become a person, one has to find the real me and get rid of all the false me's that socialization created.[13] His mantra: "To find the real me, it is necessary to jettison the law and the prophets, the New Testament, even Freud and Jung and rely on your own direct experience. All else is phoniness."

In 1976, for example, Rogers, expressing the real me inside himself, spoke of his ill wife, Helen: "If I give up my life or personhood to the care of her, then I'm going to become bitter. I am going to become angry inside at what I have given up....It would be out of a sense of duty and that isn't the kind of relationship I want."[14] In *Listening to Prozac* (1993), Peter D. Kramer says, "For Rogers, the cardinal sin in therapy, or in teaching or family life is the imposition of authority."[15]

Then there was Abraham Maslow, who felt Christianity was evil superstition. He fervently believed that individuals could be liberated through "peak experiences" and thus achieve self-actualization.[16] His idea that we were all born flawless was itself deeply flawed as his friends frequently pointed out to him. But it was very popular. As time went on, he became discouraged saying fewer and fewer (only 50 percent and then only 20 percent) were capable of self-actualization.

Maslow was convinced that the Catholic Church, among other institutions, had to go and that humanistic psychology was a perfect replacement. He writes in his diary of a talk he gave in Holy Week 1962 at Sacred Heart College in Newton, Massachusetts: "They shouldn't applaud me. They should attack. If they were fully aware of what I was doing, they would."[17] Other experts expressed similar antiauthoritarian sentiments. What was praised was the self that is authentic, unfettered by authority, unblocked, spontaneous, well developed, and liberated.

PRESENT-DAY CONSIDERATIONS

Why is authority in trouble today? Because of the "movers and shakers" who helped shape our culture in this antiauthoritarian direction. Remember Timothy Leary's mantra: Question authority.[18] The degree to which we buy into an antiauthoritarian view of life is the degree to which we become self-centered, not other-centered. A culture of egocentricity is created, a culture of "I deserve" and "I come first."

Nobody has a right to tell me I am a sinner and no one can tell me what to think or what to do. In plain words, this type of popular culture seems to invite individuals to rebellion against traditional moral values and even rebellion against God himself.

Once again, recall that much of what these authors said rang true and was helpful, but it had an antiauthoritarian core, often invisible to many people, and very destructive.

The goal of Karl Marx and Sigmund Freud, namely, to get rid of guilt, has been achieved far beyond their wildest expectations. Our culture teaches that nonconforming is a right and even a duty. Young people are made to feel accepted if they challenge authority and fear being shunned if they conform to the authority of their parents or teachers, even parents who do not abuse their powers and even teachers who do not deserve to be rejected.

It is important to remember that if negative reinforcement is to work, individuals must realize they deserve some of the troubles at their doorstep. Secular society, however, says: Negative consequences are unjustified and unfair. They are inappropriate intrusions into our lives. In other words, so many do not perceive themselves as sinful or in need of repentance, but they see themselves as victims of injustice and unfairness. Sin and repentance are not in their hearts and they resent anyone who tries to put them there.

Yet keeping people on the path of right moral behavior and off the path of sinfulness is one of the functions of authority. Yes, the job of authority is to guard boundaries in order to foster appropriate behavior such as truthfulness and honesty and diminish inappropriate behavior such as lying, cheating, and stealing. It is the duty of authority to point out there are clear limits to what the self can do. The self is not prior to or apart from certain central roles as son/daughter, mother/father, husband/wife, and so on. Bernard Lonergan often said that we are a we before we are an I.[19]

Church leaders and religious educators need to clearly impart to the faithful that there are *Ten Commandments,* not ten suggestions. If moms and dads are to be good parents they have to teach their children that stealing is wrong. Police have to enforce the laws against murder and mayhem. Teachers have to instruct children and insist that they learn even on days when they do not want to learn. Bosses have to ensure a harassment-free workplace where people must sublimate their impulses in order to work together. All these proposals are attacked or subverted by major elements of our culture.

Dana Mack wisely says this antiauthoritarian approach did not permeate all American households. "There is no doubt, however, that proponents of the therapeutic parenting model exerted an enormous influence on the best educated Americans."[20] That includes bishops, clergy, and religious. These notions of antiauthoritarianism "came to permeate education, social work and even mass media."[21]

Environmental Reinforcement and Its Effects

So authority is in trouble first and foremost because our secular culture wages war against it on many fronts. Let us try to understand this environmental reinforcement.

What is reinforcement? It is a straightforward process whereby the positive consequences for a behavior increase the likelihood that the behavior will occur in the future; negative consequences decrease that likelihood.

For example, if I am praised by my peers for defying authority, and if they look at me as a hero, this will tend in most cases to increase the future rate of my defiant behavior. That acclaim is a reinforcer. Similarly, most wise parents have found they can teach their children to engage in certain behaviors such as making their beds, cleaning their rooms, cutting the grass, and shoveling the snow if they provide something the children see as desirable as a consequence of their successful completion of the task and something negative for neglect of the task. That something is a reinforcer.

Now expand the notion of reinforcement to a whole school, a whole office building, a whole neighborhood, a whole environment reinforcing certain attitudes, feelings, and behaviors. Can this be done? Yes, and often successfully.

Evidence, for example, suggests that the environment in the higher echelons of corporations such as Enron and WorldCom was so reinforcing of lying, cheating, and stealing that it gradually influenced otherwise decent people to engage in these behaviors and call them entrepreneurial.

Our culture today has massive elements—such as music, cinema, television, the Web, and advertising—that create an almost total environment for our children and young adults and that encourage them to reject whatever authority figures have to say in order to be "cool." Being accepted by peers for being "cool" is a stronger reinforcement for some today than approval by loved ones or church leaders, so it trumps what they have to offer.

Thus there is a struggle going on in our culture for the minds and hearts of us all. Bishops, pastors, teachers, parents are subject to the same environmental forces of ridicule for being too strict, too rule bound. The message: "Don't lay a guilt trip on us. It will damage self-esteem." Moms and dads report being reluctant to discipline for fear their children will say, "I hate you," and "I am telling all my friends you are a bad mom." Parents are admonished to use a counseling approach. Educators were trained to help students achieve self-actualization. Bishops were praised for being pastoral, not in the sense of Gregory the Great's *Regula Pastoralis*, but in the Rogerian sense of unconditional positive regard.

Who invented total environmental reinforcement? Nazi Germany's propaganda minister, Josef Goebbels, and Joseph Stalin in Russia followed Goebbels's example because it worked. Goebbels was such a diabolically clever person that he had most Germans sooner or later cooperating with the Holocaust. And these had been heretofore decent Christians, mostly Roman Catholic and Lutheran.

On one hand, there was positive reinforcement consisting of multivaried rewards for following the Fuehrer. On the other hand, should you refuse to follow the Nazi ideology, the Gestapo was always there to dish out enormous pain. With such strong environmental currents, it was only a matter of time before even some ministers and priests—and bishops—were finding their latent anti-Semitic prejudices emboldened by Nazi ideology.

An example is an April 1938 statement by a priest in charge of Catholic Action in Austria: "Adherence to Aryan thought should see God's Word in Adolph Hitler's historic mission...the Jewish question has remained unresolved in history. Now it is being resolved by our Fuehrer."[22] It would take a great deal of moral courage to stand up against a whole culture and it should not be surprising that not everyone did. Think of the moral courage of Dietrich Bonhoeffer joining a plot to assassinate Hitler "to cut off the head of the snake."[23] So, too, in our time almost the whole American environment reinforces rejection of certain central Judeo-Christian teachings, feelings, and behaviors. Clergy who are praised for doing away with the idea of a divine standard of right and wrong are reinforced to do more. Those who speak seriously about hell are scorned and mocked. So strong are those currents that as far back as 1973, Karl Menninger, the famous psychiatrist, had to ask the question: *Whatever became of sin?*[24]

Feelings of anxiety and guilt are diminished by repetition of a powerful mantra: *"You have no right to make me feel that way."* For example, the secular culture appears to applaud all kinds of sexual acting out, heaping scorn on opponents and praise on those who say: God made me this way, so it cannot be wrong. This is self-absorption, which is just another name for selfishness.

Taking an Alternative Stance

The ridicule of traditional Judeo-Christian teaching especially on sexual morality so pervades our environment and daily bombards our people that some Christians have been converted by the clever lies of the media, and even some ministers and priests find their autoerotic impulses aroused by politically correct sexual ideology. It takes a great deal of courage to stand up against this and proclaim with St. Paul: "I am not ashamed of the gospel" (Rom 1:16). But political correctness does not stop there.

Many parents are bombarded by the media with the idea that discipline will have a negative impact on their children. So fathers today abandon their role as disciplinarians to become buddies of their sons, a fatal blow to fathering. Good dads used to know intuitively that one of the best reinforcers for their adolescent son's good behavior was to take their son hunting or fishing or to a ball game or a car show. Sons learned in those days that you could lose a hunting trip with dad if your behavior was unacceptable. Dad's job was to enforce the rules with rewards and punishments. But the environment today says dads should take their sons hunting and fishing no matter what their behavior is.

We see this over and over among the boys who live with us in Father Flanagan's famous village. At the insistence of our culture, their dads (when they were around) were their buddies, at times engaging in drugs and sex and alcohol with them. We see the same with our girls, whose mothers abandoned being disciplinarians and are just "good friends" to their daughters. The secular culture conditions moms and dads to act in this way.

The celebrated preacher, Robert Schuller, of the Crystal Cathedral, in 1982 published *Self-Esteem: The New Reformation*.

We have both arrived at the same bottom line: unconditional self-esteem, self-love that doesn't have to be earned because it is given....I believe that the vision that forms the core of most religious thinking has to do with joy. Unfortunately, the message gets distorted into fear, guilt and mistrust.[25]

Schuller sees this as the new reformation, throwing out mortification of self and negative emotions "from which so many suffer today."

Many good teachers know intuitively that too much praise for too little behavior is a bad idea and that a child is not going to learn without discipline. But it takes a very strong-willed teacher to go against the environment of our day and be a solid and fair disciplinarian. A principal needs to have an awful lot of courage to create a school environment where praise and rewards are contingent on real learning and upright behavior.

Our grade-school students write essays once every six weeks to develop good thought patterns and writing styles. The other day after an awards caucus, a new student raised his hand and asked why he did not get a certificate. I asked what he was thinking of. His response: "I handed in an essay so I should have an award." And when I assured him he would earn an award when he improved his style and content, he accepted it but looked at me as if I missed the point of it all.

For some, contemporary environmental reinforcement strikes a near fatal blow at healthy parenting, solid education, and respect for authority. Since church leaders do not live in a vacuum-sealed container, environmental reinforcement is as strong in their lives as elsewhere. They live in a society that bombards them with continual exhortations to quit preaching sin and just make people feel good by being pastoral. The message to preachers more often than not is that they should gloss over the Fall of Adam and Eve (our culpability, our frailty, and our need for salvation) and talk about the boundless love and affirmation God has for us all.

Pope John Paul II popularized the idea of a culture of life standing up for the poor, the needy, the aged, the newborn, and a culture of death with contraception, abortion, euthanasia, and stem-cell research. When he talked about the dignity of the human person, some in our culture missed his point and translated it into a statement in support of egocentricity, freedom from authority, and the rejection of the divine standard of right and wrong. He encouraged healthy conscience formation, but of the four elements necessary for such a conscience, two were missing in our culture, namely, guilt and shame, and all that was left was compassion and sympathy.

REASONS WHY AUTHORITY
IS IN TROUBLE

The first reason authority is in trouble is because of the multilayered cultural currents acting like an environmental Hurricane Katrina, sweeping aside authority's necessary functions.
Bernard Lonergan once said, "There is no use appealing to the sense of responsibility of irresponsible people, to the reasonableness of people that are unreasonable, to the intelligence of people who have chosen to be obtuse, to the attention of people that attend only to their grievances."[26]
The second reason why authority is in trouble is the widespread recognition that in order to keep its power, authority sometimes exaggerates. The recognition that authority often

16

exaggerates erodes credibility and is used to undermine the power of authority figures to say right is right and wrong is wrong and make it stick.

I remember as a child the stories that my parents told my brothers and myself to help us understand why there were rules such as: Eat your soup, don't play with matches, don't play in the street, and don't suck your thumb.

We were an immigrant-oriented family and we memorized certain children's poems in German. For example, little Pauline started to play with matches when her parents were out and she burned down the house. I can still see the picture of the ashes that were once Pauline. And then there was the Strubblepeter who did not eat his soup. I can still see the picture of his grave (he died of starvation) with an empty soup bowl as a monument to his foolishness.

My brothers and I lived in a culture respectful of the authority of our mom and dad. We knew they loved us and we knew the Great Depression made for very hard times. Our parents' exaggerations were not the source of anger in our hearts. And because the environment supported respect for our mom and dad and their authority, nobody made fun of them for exaggerating. Fear of playing with matches really is a healthy attitude and eating your soup is a good idea, especially because mom made lots of soup. The rules functioned well even if there were obvious exaggerations. But in our current culture, examples such as these are used to make fun of authority and to reject all use of negative consequences.

The entertainment media regularly indulges in straightforwardly crass ridicule of authority. Nothing is sacred. MTV teaches it is cool to defy authority and clearly Jackass, Muck, and Midriff are positive role models. Drugs, sex, and alcohol are all sold under the antiauthoritarian banner of being cool.

Tattoos as well as lip rings and tongue studs are all meant to thumb one's ring-filled nose at authority.

Religious authority also made exaggerated claims for certain rules in our faith lives. In the pre-Vatican II church there was a rule that we should not participate in Protestant worship services. "If you do, you may lose your faith altogether." There was a similar rule in many Protestant denominations warning them never to attend the idolatry that is called Catholic Mass.

In our Catholic tradition there was something called the *Index of Forbidden Books*. It said: If you read Karl Marx's *Das Kapital*, you may become a raving Communist. In Italy it was said that if you read the daily Communist newspaper *L'Unità*, you would be automatically excommunicated. Who knows what frightful things might happen to you if you read even a paragraph or two.

Seminary authorities often exaggerated this viewpoint by telling us: The seminary rules are the voice of God. At the time I thought it was a silly exaggeration and felt sorry for those who took it seriously, later becoming very angry at the church when they realized it was an exaggeration.

Yes, our religious leaders looked somewhat silly by claiming God's authority for these rules. But the environment in which we lived supported respect for church authority, so these exaggerations were not used as another reason to jettison respect.

We now live in a culture where these exaggerations by religious authority are used time and again to mock that same authority and insist the church has no right to make us feel guilty. Cynics use these exaggerations assuming a posture of self-righteous rejection of traditional moral norms. They focus people's anger on these exaggerations in such a way as to make authority figures look stupid. Some bishops did not, however, require outside assistance to look foolish.

The deeper the anger, the more strident the criticism, the greater the feeling of being duped and the less likely it is church authority will be respected. When church authority is made to look stupid, dissent from church teaching becomes widespread. Cardinal Dulles puts it this way: "Dissent is rampant, not only on secondary and reformable teachings, but even on central doctrines of faith."[27]

IMPACT OF SECULAR REASONS FOR REJECTING AUTHORITY

Since this is the case, there can also be wholesale rejection of the gospel authority to "teach all nations." To Peter, the Lord said: "I will give you the keys of the kingdom of heaven" (Matt 16:19). For us to sweep aside the gospel mandate because of our lousy environment means we are "ashamed of the gospel" (Rom 1:16). But with St. Paul we know in our hearts we cannot be ashamed of the gospel.

To sum up, there are strong secular reasons why authority is in trouble. Many layers of our culture teach us to reject authority. Authority figures often do err or exaggerate in their pronouncements. And of course every failing of bishops, pastors, and even the Holy Father is magnified by the media, and that reinforces the idea that we should not trust church authority. To distrust church authority means that each of us should be very suspicious about any authoritarian teaching. Who gave them the power to tell us what to do? This begets the rampant disrespect for authority Cardinal Dulles is speaking out against.

So far we have seen how first there was a frontal attack on parenting that undermined the authority of the family. We then saw how the mantra of self-fulfillment undermined church authority and church community. So now let us consider three harmful consequences that would come to anyone so wholly engulfed in these enormous cultural forces as to totally reject the church's rightful teaching authority.

Three Significant Consequences

First, wholesale rejection of church authority would separate us from the Christian community of the past. The church down through the ages was respectful and accepting of scripture and tradition, both inspired by the Holy Spirit. If we were to reject the authority of the church completely and embrace wholesale dissent, we would no longer believe what Christians of old believed and our moral teaching would be vastly different from theirs. As a result, such persons today would no longer have much in common with the martyrs and saints of old. This would be a great loss engendering loneliness, fragmentation, and separation from the body of Christ over time. We would thus be disengaged from the body of Christ over time. The inspiration and encouragement that used to flow to us from the martyrs and saints of old would be no more:

> For all the saints who from their labors rest,
> who you by faith before the world confessed;
> Thy name, O Jesus, be forever blessed!
> Alleluia, Alleluia!

For example, a complete acceptance of a theology of compromise would sever our ties with the ancient martyrs who did not compromise, dying courageously for their faith, and whose lives inspired Christians for thousands of years. To cut ourselves off from our Christian past would be much more awful than it sounds. It would be like walking away in anger from the family that nourished us from our child-hood, rendering meaningless for us their courage, their example, and their hope. The emotions of attachment and fellowship with the saints of old, as well as affection and warmth for them, would wither and die. So we would refuse to let the family that loved us and raised us love us anymore. We would be now alone with our iPods and DVDs, random isolates, unrelated to our past and emancipated from it. We would believe our teachers and parents to have been mis-guided. We would have a dissenting heart.

What we would have lost is any guidance and inspira-tion from our past. Our feeling of connectedness would be replaced by a feeling of unconnectedness and distance. Gone forever would be the happy memories helping you to look "for the silver lining when ere a cloud appears in the blue."

Think of the great saints in every age of the church who can be a source of inspiration for us if we do not dissent from everything they believed or whatever they did. They are not wax figures in a museum from a quaint historical past; or rather, they don't have to be. They are real people who can show us the beauty of our faith and the courage to live it joy-fully.

In other words, wholesale dissent tends to separate us from the Christian community of the past very much to our own detriment. There may be a few exceptions from this rule, but there are not many.

Secondly, wholesale dissent from church authority and its teaching would separate us from the church of the present. It would cause us to feel less and less part of the people of God today and more and more separated and unconnected.

Unconnected means lonely and self-absorbed. And self-absorption means self-salvation because God believes in my self-affirmation and loves me for it. I have no need of some savior to free me from myself...a savior whose name is Jesus. Perhaps I may need a self-help group. I do not need Sunday church; leave me alone.

So I would reject the announcement of the Archangel Gabriel: "[H]e will save his people from their sins" (Matt 1:21). I don't have sins, so I don't need salvation from them, but I do have a self-image that other people have wounded. What that means is that wholesale dissent would not only cut me off from my past, but also obscure my present. Loneliness and bone-chilling alienation would be my companions in a crowd of wealthy, cynical people.

One of the major themes of the scriptures is that our faith comes to us through the community of believers. Yes, you can pray on a mountaintop and yes, you can pray on your patio. But the only place you can "do this in remembrance of me" is together in church. By absenting ourselves we would be deprived of a deep sense of the sacred and we would lose the communion of the saints, the forgiveness of sins, and life everlasting. Amen.

> Amazing grace, how sweet the sound
> that saved a wretch like me.
> I once was lost, but now am found,
> was blind, but now I see.

Thirdly, wholesale dissent from church authority and its teaching would cancel out the future. I would have no hope to be with the church triumphant in heaven, namely, all my loved ones and all the saints of old. This would no longer motivate me as I have no longing to be "with the Lord." The vision of the

22

barque of Peter carrying us over the stormy seas to the Promised Land would be only a Renaissance painting in the Vatican Museum and nothing more. Being with my loved ones in heaven would be an empty phrase. *"Spes nostra, salve"* would mean nothing. I would be an empty self with no past, no future, and only an isolated present. Christians in ages past used to share St. Paul's intense desire for heaven. But I would lose that desire when I allowed dissent to capture my heart. This old hymn would no longer move my soul:

> Swing low, sweet chariot, coming for to carry me home;
> Swing low, sweet chariot, coming for to carry me home.
> I looked o're Jordan, and what did I see, coming for to carry me home?
> A band of angels coming after me, coming for to carry me home.
> Swing low, sweet chariot.

Psychologist Paul Vitz rightly points out that once you abandon the blessedness of heaven, namely, the Christian vision of human fulfillment as union with God and others in him, then you do not look outside yourself for fulfillment but rather inward.[28] You would replace the Christian vision with the secular view of fulfillment as the search for self-satisfaction and self-achievement. The self would become the center of all your desiring and the road to this self-fulfillment would be quite obviously a different road from the road to heaven.

SOME CONCLUDING POINTS
TO CONSIDER

If we do not want to lose our energizing connection with the Christian past, our sense of being part of the people of God today, and our intense desire for heaven in the future, then we must fight against this secular challenge to authority.

O God, our help in ages past,
our hope for years to come,
our shelter from the stormy blast,
and our eternal home.

Under the shadow of your throne,
your saints have dwelt secure.
Sufficient is your arm alone,
and our defense is sure.

Before the hills in order stood,
or earth received its frame,
from everlasting you are God,
to endless years the same.

A thousand ages in your sight
are like an evening gone,
short as the watch that ends the night,
before the rising sun.

There are four new tasks for those who would respond to this challenge and renew themselves in the church.

1. Develop a slightly countercultural lifestyle symbolized by the expression: *"I am a citizen of Heaven."* Avoid

the secular rejection of authority and be polite about it. Learn to trust God's holy scriptures and tradition, both inspired by the Holy Spirit. They are the words of eternal life. Ask God daily to cleanse your heart and lips that you may worthily proclaim his gospel by your daily living.

2. Learn to trust authority when trust is warranted and to distrust authority when distrust is warranted. Build a warranted trust of the hierarchy.

3. Teach your family and friends how environmental reinforcement shapes our thoughts, feelings, and behaviors. Help them to enjoy the good things of the earth as God's gifts. Help them to learn not to believe everything they see on TV or read in the newspapers. Inspire them to embrace the passion, death, and resurrection of Jesus and share in them. Show them the beauty of God's word and sacraments so they may call good good and evil evil. Be proud that your family is not a bunch of followers. "We are different."

4. Add to the good current cultural focus on compassion and sympathy a healthy gospel-based sense of appropriate guilt and shame. It worked for King David and St. Peter. It can work for us.

Chapter 2

RELIGIOUS REASONS FOR WHY AUTHORITY IS IN TROUBLE

In the previous chapter, we considered two secular reasons why authority is in trouble today, why there is so much dissent, and how this negativity affects our faith lives. This chapter will consider religious reasons, once again preparing ourselves to respond positively, affirmatively, and therapeutically. In a culture where authority is so roundly chastised, our task is counterintuitive, namely, to show how healthy authority can be a powerful influence in our attempts to live the gospel ideals.

SOME INITIAL CONSIDERATIONS

First, we pointed to several contemporary cultural currents that are trying their best to extinguish in us sentiments of guilt and shame while ridiculing those in authority whose job it is to call right *right* and wrong *wrong*. The need to resist steadfastly those cultural currents was stressed. Popular parenting experts and prominent psychologists were cited. How authority sometimes exaggerates, in order to keep its power, was then considered. The need to understand that exaggeration and not to overreact or make dishonoring authority a way of life was stressed. Finally, what happens to a person who, caught up in these oppositional defiant currents, ends up with an attitude of wholesale dissent was illustrated.

The days of Vatican II were indeed exhilarating for the Catholic Church in America. Blessed Pope John XXIII told us to open the windows and let the fresh air of modern times into our lives and our church. During that time many read Harvey Cox's *The Secular City*[1] like enthusiastic adolescents enjoying a newfound freedom. Many religious leaders helped steer the barque of Peter into these new cultural channels.

In this chapter we point to a third and fourth reason why authority is in trouble today. These are religious in nature. They are the loss of a sense of sin on one hand and on the other the loss of so much of the church's credibility in the recent sexual abuse crisis highlighted by a seemingly anti-Catholic attitude in much media coverage.

The Loss of Sin

The third factor so influential in our environment today is the loss of the sense of original sin and personal sin. Within a culture of searching for our true self, it is as if the long-cherished idea of sin challenges our sense of individual freedom and openness and honesty.

In 1969, Sheed and Ward translated a 1966 German work of Herbert Haag, *Is Original Sin in Scripture?*[2] Bruce Vawter, the popular biblical scholar, wrote the introduction. Haag's resounding answer to the question was no.

In his summary, Haag says:

The research presented above has the following consequences: (1) The idea that Adam's descendents are automatically sinners because of the sin of their ancestor and that they are already sinners when they enter the world, is foreign to Holy Scripture. (2) The inheritance of Adam's sin means rather that…all men are born into a sinful world and in this sinful world become themselves sinners. (3) No man enters the world a sinner. As the creature and image of God, he is from the first hour surrounded by God's fatherly love.…A man becomes a sinner only through his own individual and responsible action.[3]

This thinking was repeated by many similar-minded scholars and gained such popularity that what we see today is the widespread, pervasive belief that we are born with a clean slate, with no inherent proclivity to evil, no moral weaknesses, and no inner dividedness. Remember this is exactly what our humanist psychologist friends cited in the prior chapter were saying as well. In this view, all the troubles besetting us are the result of influences outside of us, starting at our birth with misuse of authority, poor parenting, poor schooling, poverty, prejudice, injustice, and so much else.

Today in American management theory, there has been much talk about the silo effect and the stovepiping of issues. If a corporation's design team, production team, and marketing division do not interact (all live in silos) and they stovepipe their recommendations to top management, chaos can occur. For our purposes, this simply means that scripture scholars were in one silo, moralists were in another, humanistic psychologists in another. And these silos were stovepiping their material up to clergy, religious, and laity, who often lacked the critical tools of discernment.

In addition, scripture scholars began to understand literary forms, symbolic language, and mythic truths and popularized their findings with the sincere hope that this would enrich people and make the scriptures come alive for us. In some ways an opposite result occurred as more people seemed to side with the psychologists who downplayed traditional religion altogether.

At the same time, there came to the fore in America a two-story concept of truth where the lower story of the house is occupied by the *objective truth* of the empirical sciences and technology.[4] The second floor is home to our *subjective personal truths* about religion and spirituality.

Church scholars living in separate silos have unwittingly fostered the relegation of sin to the second floor with their notions of myth (the Flood), symbol (Adam and Eve), and metaphor (the Creation story).

The task before us is to affirm the teaching of the church on original sin while at the same time seeking a way to weave this teaching into good, solid notions of literary forms and symbolic language in order to truly make the scriptures come alive for us. The result for too many faithful has been just the opposite: Why bother reading the scriptures because they are too complicated and only scholars can understand what they mean?

A second example is the widespread loss of a sense of serious personal sin. It can be illustrated by an otherwise unexceptional book by Sean Fagan, *Has Sin Changed?*[5] The author has no intention of "doing away with the notion of sin or in any way minimizing its importance," and yet that is what he does unwittingly through stovepiping the issue with a silo effect. Fagan asks: Are there things that we should never do that are always wrong? His answer: "The vain search for absolute moral truths is part of the human lust for certainty."[6] What about mortal and venial sin? Fagan: "Today's Catholics no longer accept such a simple rule of thumb."[7] He says, "Modern psychology has added several nuances."[8] What about guilt? "Psychiatrists can tell of the high percentage of their patients who are crippled by a burden of neurotic guilt that has little to do with real sin and moral conscience."[9] The author has a whole chapter on "How sinful is sex?" Not very. He acknowledges "the worldwide decline of respect for authority" without recognizing that, through siloing, he is increasing this worldwide decline.[10]

One of my teachers from the past, Bernard J. F. Lonergan, SJ, popularized the notion of horizon analysis or what is called a worldview. The worldview of so much popular culture today is that sacred things are personal, subjective truths and the secular things are objective truths. I am arguing that our task is to liberate the Catholic Church in America from this cultural captivity.

Lonergan described sin as "alienation from man's authentic being, which is self-transcendence and sin justices itself by ideology."[11] Original sin is a statistical probability in the moral order that is inherent in each of us. In other words, given enough instances of activity, it is inevitable that the flaws that are passed on to us from Adam and Eve will result in personal sin. Although the secular culture describes this view as our personal, subjective truth, it seems quite the contrary to be first-story objectivity and not some prejudice within ourselves.

According to Romans 5:12, the power of sin effects in every one of us a ratification of Adam's rebellion against

God. That universal power first asserted itself in his disobedience. Tribute is paid to it in our lives, for we are born into it and ratify it with personal sin.

The *Catechism of the Catholic Church* says it this way: "As a result of original sin, human nature is weakened in its power; subject to ignorance, suffering, and the domination of death; and *inclined to sin.*"[12]

The *Catechism* continues: "Christians believe that the world has been established and kept in being by the Creator's love; has fallen into slavery to sin but has been set free by Christ, crucified and risen to break the power of the evil one."[13]

The good news in our lives is in response to this bad news. The *Catechism* says that "as a result of original sin...human nature is subject to ignorance."[14] So part of the bad news is that as a result of original sin some get things like love all mixed up. It is true, for example, that God loves us always, even when we sin. But some do not know that and so they believe they have to earn God's love or merit it. Once they sinned, Adam and Eve hid themselves from God; and with what they had done, they could not longer feel God's love, even though it was still there. And not feeling it they thought they had to merit it, so they hid themselves because they knew they could not merit it.

Some of my Boys Town kids have stayed away from religion because they felt they must merit God's love, but how is that possible with such a shattered past? Meriting God's love is self-salvation. On the other hand, these kids are in the minority today when so many other kids fall into the opposite error, namely, that God loves them so much that there is no sin. They feel they may make mistakes and errors by doing drugs or shoplifting, but that's it. Yes, environmental conditioning is that strong.

Part of the bad news of original sin is bodily death. St. Paul calls death "the wages of sin." As we experience it, it truly is bad news. We first experience it when we are young on the occasion of a tragic loss of our loved ones. As we grow older the dread of its coming upon us is enormous, and, since our postmodern world scoffs at the resurrection, death is perfumed and dressed up. Progressives endeavor to make a funeral a totally joy-filled event rather than the bittersweet experience our heart tells us it is.

Difference between Sin and Error

Judeo-Christian morality teaches us there is a difference between sin and error. If you say 2+2=5, that is an error, not a sin. If you say you did not steal when you did, that is a sin, not an error. If you commit adultery, that is a sin, not an error. Our culture wants to explain all human aberrations as errors and mistakes but not sins. So when pastors or religion teachers today say one commits a sin by lying, cheating, or stealing, they are looked upon as quaint and old-fashioned, living on the second story of our house. Today if your pastor says you are living in sin, he is often ridiculed, mocked, and treated with great disrespect.

The truth is this: If you believe 2+2=5, then you need a little lesson in mathematics, a little education. Yes, your error is corrected through education. If you commit adultery, the remedy is repentance, not education. Why? Because committing adultery is a sin, not an error, and the remedy for sin is repentance, just as the remedy for error is education.

Now let us say you have a culture like ours, which tries to eliminate all sin. Then you will see more and more people thinking they are only making mistakes. And you will have more and more people believing that education, not repentance, is the key to all betterment of the human race.

If we live in a culture that suggests nobody is a sinner, then we are all merely people who make mistakes. So all we need is more education, more seminars, more self-help groups, more diversity training, and more learning experiences. So we need therapists, not confessors. We need facilitators for group work, not saints. Interestingly enough, the gospels do not talk about therapists or facilitators; they talk about saints and sinners.

St. Paul says it well: "[A]ll have sinned and fall short of the glory of God" (Rom 3:23). Our culture would have us glory in our self-esteem; St. Paul would have us "never boast of anything except the cross of our Lord Jesus Christ" (Gal 6:14).

CRISIS OF CHURCH'S CREDIBILITY

The fourth factor in the changed environment is the crisis inside the American Catholic Church. The recent clerical sexual-abuse scandal and cover-up have contributed significantly to this changed environment. There is an old Latin phrase, *corruptio optimi pessima*, which means the worst corruption is that of one on a pedestal. The vast majority of American Catholics have been scandalized beyond belief and rightly so. Margaret O'Brien Steinfels told the bishops in Dallas: "We must recognize that what has happened is a terrible blow to the Church's witness in a culture, a blow to its credibility in proclaiming the good news...."[15]

Bitter anti-Catholics in the media ask us straightforwardly: "Why, for heaven sakes, would you stay in the church? Why would you work for renewal and reform when some of your leaders have failed you grievously with grossly immoral actions, and then copped a plea by apologizing for 'errors of judgment,' instead of repenting for their sins and thinking things are back to normal when they have done so? Why would you stay?"

Henri de Lubac, in a little book entitled *Further Paradoxes* (1958), says:

> I have been told that a young intelligent priest, full of good qualities, has left the Church and apostatized, declaring he was scandalized by certain attitudes on the part of the hierarchy. I am not interested in what these attitudes were. I am willing to grant, as a hypothesis, with my eyes shut, that these attitudes were in fact regrettable. I am even willing to imagine worse ones. But what was this young priest's faith, then, before the disaster happened? What was his idea of the Church? What consciousness had he of the life he received from it and what esteem for it? And did he know so little of its history? One cannot wonder that his experience was brief; had he never read in his breviary the homily where St. Gregory explains that you must not expect to find a domain without scandals before the coming of the Kingdom?
>
> Even should St. Paul, at the time of the conflict at Antioch, have had twenty times more to complain about…that the attitude adopted by the pillars of the Church were twenty times more scandalous, can it be imagined that his faith in Christ would have been the least bit shaken? Or that the scandal would have been capable of alienating him, however slightly, from the one Church of Christ? Our faith is the same today, the foundations are the

same, it has been kindled at the same hearth, the same Spirit continues to infuse it in our hearts.[16]

The fathers of the church pointed out that God took Israel as an adulterous bride, the way the prophet Hosea (Osee) was told by God to take Gomer as his bride and remain faithful to her in spite of her adultery.

REASONS FOR REMAINING IN A SINFUL CHURCH

Why would you stay? For the same reasons that Paul stayed when Peter sinned. As members of the fallen human race, we need the church and cannot save ourselves. We need the church to preach the gospel faithfully and to administer the sacraments rightly. So we need to help purify our beloved family of God, the church. Cardinal Avery Dulles wisely says, "To be Catholic is precisely to see one's self as part of a greater whole, to be inserted in the Church universal."[17]

I know of people who have left the church and tried to make it on their own. So many of these are well-intentioned people who are "fed up" with the scandals and with the progressive and conservative church battles of the last three or four decades. Many who leave are glad to be rid of all the politics and yet they are still sad at heart, going it alone. When they see no purification, reform, or renewal, they lose heart.

They instinctively feel the need for the gospel to be preached authentically; they do not want ideology of either the left or the right. They miss the Mass and holy communion, and all the sacraments. They do not just want preaching about Jesus, they hunger for Jesus himself as the eucharistic food for the journey.

Why does the church need renewal? For persons like these among others. For the church is God's chosen instrument of salvation, at once holy and sinful, founded by God's Son on the faith of Peter and the apostles.

Why else do we need the church? For that multitude of faith-filled people who have not left, who hunger for the Bread of Life, who love the ancient faith, who recognize all of us as suffering from the scandals, the materialism, selfishness, mistrust, and inability to love, and who are hanging on. All these scourges are characteristics of our age, and the multitude of faith-filled people is clinging to the Lord and his church as the only hope of rescue from shipwreck.

Faith ennobles them, hope encourages them, and charity beckons to them. They need and deserve a reformed church. Think of the church the way St. John Chrysostom did, as the donkey that carried Jesus into Jerusalem on Palm Sunday. Down through the ages the donkey plods along bringing us Jesus through word and sacrament as food for the journey to heaven. Every fifty years or so we look at the treasure chest the donkey is carrying on its back and, opening it, discover some of the church's riches for our time. In traditional iconography the donkey is God's holy creature that carried Mary to Bethlehem. It is the beloved creature that carries Jesus to us in every age; the donkey is not free from original sin.

So it is clear why we should stay in the church: for the same reasons St. Paul stayed in the church; for the same reasons Henri de Lubac stayed in the church; for the same reasons St. Francis of Assisi stayed in the church; for the same reasons St. Ignatius of Loyola and St. Catherine of Siena stayed.

ADDITIONAL CONSIDERATIONS

The media had a heyday several years ago when certain self-righteous evangelical leaders of the religious right were caught in the act of lusting after money, power, and sex and exposed them as religious frauds. Their sins did much to reinforce the idea that the religious right should not be listened to because their religion was untrustworthy and to be banished from the public forum. But there was an equal if not greater joy and delight at the terrible scandals of Catholic priest abusers.

Remember that anti-Catholicism also needs to be factored in to the scandalous loss of credibility in the church. Ken Woodward, who for thirty-eight years was religion editor at *Newsweek*, writes:

> Has some of the coverage of the current scandal in the Catholic Church been driven by anti-Catholicism?
>
> Indeed, in style, intensity, and the unrelenting nature of the coverage, some of it has. ABC's Prime Time News Special "Father Forgive Me for I Have Sinned" is a prominent example of what happens when producers choose a story line beforehand and use only the interview material that furthers it. Peter Jennings, who is usually sensitive to religious nuance, should have known better. Similar examples could be drawn from *Vanity Fair* which, especially under Tina Brown, has been unblushingly anti-Catholic to such an extent that its editors must assume that the magazine's readers are too.
>
> And then there is the *New York Times*. Compared to the way the current crisis in the Catholic Church

has been covered by, say, the *Los Angeles Times,* the coverage in the *New York Times* has been excessive and almost gleeful, revisiting old stories when no fresh news has been forthcoming and even treating parish councils as if they were radical innovations. No editor in his right mind would have printed the rant a while back by columnist Bill Keller, in which he likened Pope John Paul II to Leonid Brezhnev, unless the editor—Howell Raines—were himself anti-Catholic. It says much about the newsroom culture of the *Times* that it finds the views of a bitter ex-Catholic worth featuring on the op-ed page.[18]

Yet a free country with a free press is a blessing. And so when there is scandal, it is important for the free press to report it. If awful things have happened it is important to find out the truth and clean it up. But if there is no belief in original sin then Catholic-bashing reporters will even more inflame our anti-institutional sentiments. "The Church richly deserves to be swept away in the revolution heralding a new era." The Nazi Party publication *Durchbruch* said the same thing in the 1937 aftermath of the immorality trials.[19] St. Paul had different advice: "Do not be overcome by evil, but overcome evil with good" (Rom 12:21).

If you do not believe in original sin it comes as a great shock to discover your bishop or pastor or spiritual leader has done bad things. The *Catechism of the Catholic Church* says, "All members of the Church, including her ministers, must acknowledge that they are sinners."[20] And it makes all of us cynical when the same pastors or bishops talk to their people about doing God's will when just the opposite is happening in their lives. What shall we do? Be overcome by evil or overcome evil by doing good?

On the evening news one night, the broadcaster had just told a sordid tale about a well-respected religious leader who had embezzled some money. He asked the minister being interviewed: How could such a person of God do such a thing? The minister simply mumbled something unintelligible. He should have said: The answer is easy. It's called original sin. It is a factor in the lives of all of us.

A Consideration of Original Sin

Christians of the past two thousand years have traditionally seen human life hanging in the balance between sin and redemption. Original sin helps explain why even basically good people have a dark side. Redemption by the Lord explains why original sin is not just an excuse for not trying. With God's grace, we must overcome evil by doing good.

What is this inherent weakness in us, this original sin? It is the fact that when we are born into this world we do not have a perfectly clean slate. We are not Rousseau's noble savages, but children of Adam and Eve, their sons and daughters. Within us there is a tendency not just to good but also to evil. We do not feel God's presence as Adam and Eve did when he walked with them in the garden, for we are alienated from God. Yet we did not cause the alienation. Within us is a tendency to self-absorption that lies alongside the impulse of God's grace to self-donation. Sometimes we indulge the tendency to self-absorption, and when we do, that is actual sin. Then we believe all sorts of the devil's lies about God's love.

All we have to do is take a look at little children playing to see original sin at work. Here is one child grabbing a toy from another and over there is a child refusing to share. On the other side of the room is a child hitting another without provocation. And then there are two kids having temper tantrums.

Alongside these are touching moments of loving, little kisses and hugs, generous sharing, giving and not counting the cost.

It may be pleasing to think we are born into the world in an unspoiled state of complete innocence. But the evidence points in the opposite direction. Half our chromosomes come from our mother and the other half from our father, and we inherit from a gigantic gene pool. Even healthy babies have their troubles and if that is true on the physiological and neurological levels, why should it not be true on the psychological and spiritual levels?

As presented in the previous chapter, for the last fifty years a variety of humanistic psychologies also played a role in convincing many Americans there is no such thing as original or personal sin. Remember what Abraham Maslow said in 1955: "I sometimes think the world will be saved by psychologists—in the very broadest sense—or it will not be saved at all."[21]

Some Practical Considerations

Before concluding this chapter, some practical steps are suggested that one can take when our spiritual leaders are discovered to be engaging in misuse of their power. Let us start with relatively petty ways they might do so by acting arrogant and telling all sorts of little lies. This, of course, is a rude awakening to many because ministers, bishops, priests, and religious leaders are expected to live by a higher calling. It is shocking unless one recalls that the statistical probabilities would indicate, given enough instances, that some in that position will at times do things to be ashamed of like telling petty lies or acting pompous or being egotistical. This is part of the frailty of the human condition. But when that happens, if we do not expect it, then we are angered and scandalized and we begin to lose respect for authority. We begin to be "overcome by evil."

If we allow this to grate on us enough, we may begin to resent our spiritual leaders due to these flaws and failings. We may become cynical, having forgotten that they are part of poor fallen humankind in desperate need of salvation.

We should expect our religious leaders to strive for sanctity and achieve as a minimum a relatively high level of moral decency. This minimum standard should be, and is, a higher standard for them than for ordinary people for the simple reason that it is part of their calling to be special role models. When religious leaders fail the test of moral seriousness, they should not be allowed to get away with it. The resignation of the new archbishop of Warsaw is an example. In law it is called disbarment and in medicine it is called revocation of your license to practice medicine.

The remedy for misguided trust in authority figures is to insist on purification, reform, and renewal. This starts with developing a set of realistic criteria for trusting those who are in power. Start by replacing unconditional trust in religious leaders with merited trust. This constitutes a monumental change in our expectations. Jesus told us that "you will know them by their fruits" (Matt 7:20). A person does not consult a doctor without asking others about the doctor's reputation. If we do this with physicians why not do the same with our religious leaders? We should expect them to be people who strive for sanctity on one hand and on the other hand we should not expect them to be flawless. They

41

need to merit our trust by acting in trustworthy ways so that over time we find them trustworthy. This is the way we learn to trust other human beings. There is every reason to be just as careful here. If a physician crosses the line and practices bad medicine, we avoid that person as someone not worthy of trust. The same should be true of our religious leaders. They have bad days just as well as we do and are frail, fragile, sinful human beings. It is important to point that out because what we point out is original sin and actual sin at work in their lives just as it is in ours.

STEPS FOR RENEWAL AND PURIFICATION

This chapter concludes by suggesting an agenda we all might profitably work on if we seek renewal and purification in the church:

- We need to educate ourselves on how our faith can be enriched rather than impoverished by our postmodern culture. We need to find a way through this maze.[22]
- We need to enrich humanistic psychology with our sacred tradition. What happened that human beings, who are the great masterpiece of God's creation, have been messed up in their lives so badly? What is wrong with us? What is the source of evil and suffering?
- We can start here with the *Catechism of the Catholic Church* with its clear and concise summary of the teaching of scripture and tradition on sin and redemption. It is profitable for us to meditate on St. Paul's Epistle to the Romans, especially chapter 5.

- We need to learn what can be done to rejoice as St. Paul rejoiced in the midst of all his troubles. Here we need to focus on the death and resurrection of Jesus as a remedy for our troubles and the call for us to cooperate with the Holy Spirit in "renewing the face of the earth." This is not just religious or spiritual renewal. We do not live in a two-story house, so intellectual life needs renewal, just as political life, social life, sexual life, and so on, all need renewal. A good example here is Pope John Paul II's *Veritatis splendor*. How do we teach children and adults a Christian worldview in contrast to a postmodern secular worldview?

- In the next chapter we will see how to replace unconditional trust with merited trust in our religious leaders. The Lord himself gave us the hierarchical structure of the church, so let us embrace it wholeheartedly, while at the same time remembering the words of the Lord for those who occupy these offices: "[Y]ou will know them by their fruits" (Matt 7:20).

It took fifty to seventy-five years for the sixteenth century Counter-Reformation of the Council of Trent to become widespread. We should not expect much greater speed in our day, but the time to get started is now.

Henri Daniel-Rops makes a very interesting point in saying that reform and renewal do not have to start bottom up. They can even start with Rome. He says, "Here is another fact of capital importance. Thanks to pre-Gregorian popes, reform was carried out not in spite of Rome, as was to happen in the sixteenth century, but through her."[23] May we pray that our Holy Father, Benedict XVI, will ignite the fires of reform, purification, and renewal in this regard.

43

It is helpful to remember that, in the eleventh-century reform movement and the sixteenth-century Counter-Reformation, there was a large majority of good, faithful, and honest priests and bishops who embraced the traditional gospel message and its moral implications and who led exemplary lives. The faithful clergy greatly outnumber the unfaithful in our own day as well. We need to call on them to be in the forefront of renewal.

Likewise, recall that in Nazi Germany, where Josef Goebbels invented modern environmental reinforcement, it took a great deal of courage for clergy to stand up against a whole totalitarian culture. And some of them did have that courage, standing up in big and little ways, to Hitler, Nazism, and the destruction of the Jews.

Think of the many priests and religious in Poland and other Soviet bloc countries who withstood harassment and torture by the secret police to maintain their integrity and fidelity. Father Tadeusz Zaleski is a good example.[24]

In summary, we have to stop saying with the culture: *"Listen, Lord, your servant is speaking."* And with the saints and martyrs of old, we have to say: *"Speak Lord, your servant is listening."*

Chapter 3

*H*EALTHY *R*ESPECT
FOR AUTHORITY

In the previous two chapters we considered how authority is undermined over and over again in our present culture. Now it is time to make some basic distinctions as the groundwork (only a start) to neutralize these adverse effects and initiate a program of exceptional power for our spiritual lives. These distinctions are at the heart of renewal of rightful authority in the church.

THE SEQUESTRATION OF AUTHORITY

Sequestration is the process of delineating and separating spheres of authority and understanding how they operate. To separate spheres of authority is to diminish anger, put responsibility where it truly lies, and increase loyalty. Thirteen distinctions will be made in this chapter.

1. There is a difference between God and the church.

God is the source of all holiness, all goodness, all truth, and all beauty. God can neither deceive nor be deceived. Our human minds and hearts always fall short of the mystery of

God's holiness. In contrast to God, who is all holy, the church is not all holy even though it is the place where holiness most especially dwells. In contrast to God, who is goodness itself, the church is not all good, even though it is the place where God's goodness most especially dwells. In contrast to God, who is all beautiful, the church is not all beautiful even though it is the place where beauty most especially dwells. In contrast to God, who is truth itself, the church is not all filled with truth even though it is the place where his truth most fully dwells. We are created in the image of God's beauty and the church is the people of God. St. Thérèse of Lisieux says: "If the Church is a body composed of different members…it must have a Heart and a Heart burning with love. And I realized that this love alone was the true motive force which enabled the members of the Church to act. If it ceased to function, the Apostles would forget to preach the Gospel. The martyrs would refuse to shed their blood."[1]

As the bride of Christ the church is loved by the Lord who handed himself over for her, to purify her by his blood. The *Catechism* cites Vatican II: "The Church, however clasping sinners to her bosom, at once holy and always in need of purification/reform, follows constantly the path of penance and renewal. All members of the Church including her ministers must acknowledge that they are sinners. In everyone the weeds of sin will still be mixed with the good seed of the Gospel until the end of time. Hence the Church gathers sinners already caught up in Christ's salvation but still on the way to holiness."[2]

So the church is identified with us human beings desperately in need of the Lord's forgiveness and healing as together we walk the road of salvation.

The church can do many hurtful actions. However, it is not God who does them. It is the church and we have to accept that. Do not confuse the church with God or Jesus Christ. This is our first major distinction and it is one that will help us set proper expectations.

The Catholic Church in America today is made up by and large of good-hearted, well-intentioned human beings, some of whom, including church leaders, are too often led to believe (by powerful environmental reinforcement) that they are not obligated to walk the road of our traditional Christian creed and morality. Since the prevailing societal attitude appears to be a guilt-free one, they don't feel any guilt, much less shame, while many other Catholics are scandalized by their behavior.

It is good to recall that in World War II there were many Christians, including bishops, living in Germany who succumbed to the environmental reinforcement of the Nazi propaganda minister, Josef Goebbels, and aided in the Holocaust. Many other German Christians were rightly scandalized when Cardinal Innitzer of Vienna walked down the street to congratulate Hitler personally and welcome him on the occasion of the 1938 Anschluss when Austria became part of the Greater German Reich.

We were also rightly scandalized when our church leaders countenanced horrible things. The culture of Nazi Germany was a culture of fear-based conformity. Our culture is a culture of guilt-free self-importance. Too often people during World War II mistakenly followed Hitler instead of the Lord. Too many of our brothers and sisters today in America have mistakenly engaged in worship of the individual instead of worship of the Lord.

As the *Catechism* says, "All members of the Church, including her ministers, must acknowledge they are sinners,"[3] so we need to learn how to live in a church in which everyone is imperfect and, at the same time, hold our bishops and priests to a higher standard. We need to encourage them and support them in doing good. We need to give them strong negative feedback when necessary. Even though it is not easy it is important.

2. Not all anger is wrong. Some is righteous anger.

In St. John's account of the cleansing of the Temple, Jesus did not say, "My dearly beloved buyers and sellers, what you are doing seems inappropriate for such a holy place. Please reconsider." No, John says, "Making a whip of cords, he drove all them out of the temple, both the sheep and the cattle. He also poured out the coins of the money changers and overturned their tables. He told those who were selling the doves, 'Take these things out of here! Stop making my Father's house a marketplace!'" (John 2:15–16).

Is it permissible at times to become angry at the priests or the bishop or the pope or some other religious leader? Is there such a thing as righteous anger? The answer of course is yes. Indeed sometimes it is a good idea. Why? Because leaders such as priests or bishops or even the pope sometimes commit actions and do things that may be harmful or hurtful to the faithful. An important distinction needs to be made between the divine and human aspects of the institutional church. Ecclesiastical bureaucracy and officialdom are human aspects, where anger may be an important response. The church, founded by Christ, is God's instrument of salvation for us. Through the church the gospel is preached to us; and no matter how poorly it is preached, it is the gospel that we hear if we have ears to listen. Remember again Paul's word about the gospel: "[I]t is the power of God for salvation" (Rom 1:16).

The recent clerical sexual-abuse scandal in this country and the way it was handled have compromised the church's credibility. At times, the reputation of the institutional church suffers as a result of the actions of the small number of those actually involved. People are rightly outraged by these actions. They need to know they have a right to be angry.

Jesus did not cover up the betrayal of Judas and his subsequent despair. He is remembered as having said, "It would have been better for that one not to have been born" (Matt 26:24). Judas's betrayal is bad enough, but his despair and not turning to the Lord for forgiveness is what made it most awful. In other words, not trusting the love and power of the Lord to reach even into this darkness is frightening in all its depth.

Apart from instances of gross abuse, it is important not to stay angry long. Why? Because it will destroy you spiritually, psychologically, and in every way. A good Jewish friend of mine, born in Cologne, Germany, was sent to Auschwitz where her whole family perished and she alone survived. I once asked her how she could be so cheerful in view of all that was done to her and her loved ones. I will never forget her reply: "If I were to open my heart to anger just an inch, I would have room for nothing else. I have to fight it every day."

3. The Holy Father is the successor of Peter, not Christ.

The pope wears the shoes of the fisherman and is a mere mortal like you and me. It is anti-Catholic propaganda to say we accept the pope as Jesus' successor.

It is important to understand that Peter is called the vicar of Christ. A vicar is an agent, an administrative deputy, a stand-in, and that means he is not the real thing, just a stand-in, important as that function is. He is someone who has charge of a mission with broad pastoral responsibility. And so the word *vicar* is a good definition of Peter and those who wear the shoes of the fisherman. It is Peter's faith ("You are the Messiah, the Son of the living God") that makes the

Lord say, "[O]n this rock I will build my church" (Matt 16:16–18). It is this trust in Christ as the Messiah, the Son of the living God, that makes the pope a vicar and a pastor of us all. He is our leader in the faith. He is subject to the laws of God, not above them.

It is important to note that Vatican II documents also calls bishops "vicars of Christ."[4] So Peter is not the only vicar, but he is a special vicar in the sense that it is his kind of faith in the person of the Lord as Messiah upon which the Lord built his church.

4. It is also important to remember that there are two sides to St. Peter and his successors, acting either as Peter or as Simon.

On one hand, when the Holy Father does the will of the Lord, he is acting as Peter, declaring, "You are the Messiah, the Son of the living God." And we are to follow his example. For upon this faith, says Jesus, "I will build my church, and the gates of Hades will not prevail against it" (Matt 16:18). It is the faith that Jesus is Savior and Lord upon which the Church is built and that is the faith which you and I must embrace. It is that faith which Peter brings to us through the preaching of the Word and the administering of the sacraments. So when his successors, the popes, act with this faith, you and I must open our hearts and embrace that faith.

St. Paul says it well: "And how are they to believe in one of whom they have never heard? And how are they to hear without someone to proclaim him? And how are they to proclaim him unless they are sent?" (Rom 10:14–15).

But there are times when Peter was a scandal, an obstacle to Jesus' mission. When the Lord said he had to go to Jerusalem to suffer and to die and be raised again on the third day, Simon counseled against it. At this, Jesus said to him, "Get behind me, Satan! For you are setting your mind not on divine things but on human things" (Mark 8:33). "Simon, Simon, listen! Satan has demanded to sift all of you like wheat" (Luke 22:31). Simon at times is not acting as the vicar of Christ but rather is acting as Simon, the one who will deny the Lord three times (Mark 14:30 and Luke 22:57). We are not to follow him.

So when the Holy Father affirms our faith in Jesus as Savior and Lord, he is acting as a successor of Peter, a role model for us. But when he becomes an obstacle to the faith, as some popes did in the Middle Ages, each of these popes is acting as Simon. It can happen in any age. In both cases, it is one and the same person who wears the shoes of the fisherman. When he acts as Simon, we must avoid his bad example and his bad role modeling, for he too is a sinner like us in desperate need of salvation.

This distinction between times when the Holy Father acts as Peter and as Simon is one of the most important internal limits on his own pastoral office. It is based on scripture and not political theory. He is not a king, for a king can order his subjects at times to do things that are morally right and at times to do things that are morally wrong. And failure to obey an immoral order of a king, as in the case of St. Thomas More, means that the king's subject will be taken to Tower Hill and beheaded.

5. There are also two sides to the apostles and their successors: when they act as successors of the apostles or of Judas.

The *Catechism* says, "The bishops should not be thought of as Vicars of the Pope."[5] They are the successors of the apostles.

The *Catechism of the Catholic Church* reminds us that bishops have "as their first task to preach the Gospel of God to all in keeping with the Lord's command."[6] Citing Vatican

II, it continues, "They are heralds of faith who draw new disciples to Christ. They are authentic teachers of the apostolic faith endowed with the authority of Christ."[7]

The Lord told them, "Go therefore and make disciples of all nations" (Matt 28:19). So when they preach the gospel and when they are heralds of Christ, they are to be shown great reverence and obedience. Why? Because it is the gospel they bring that you and I must embrace. This faith they bring to us through the preaching of the word and the celebration of the sacraments.

But just as the pope either acts as Peter or as Simon, so, too, bishops act as either successors of the apostles or as successors of Judas.

In the first chapter of the Acts of the Apostles at the ascension of the Lord, Peter says of Judas, "[H]e was numbered among us and was allotted his share in this ministry" (Acts 1:17, citing Psalm 68). Judas was a scandal, an obstacle to Jesus' mission as Messiah and Lord. When the bishops act as an obstacle to Jesus' mission as Messiah and Lord, they are not acting as successors of the apostles but rather they are acting as successors of Judas, the son of perdition, who betrayed the Lord and hanged himself.

In the first chapter of Acts we read: "In those days Peter stood up among the believers…and said, 'Friends, the scripture had to be fulfilled…concerning Judas, who became a guide for those who arrested Jesus….So one of the men who have accompanied us during all the time that the Lord Jesus went in and out among us…one of these must become a witness with us of his resurrection.'…And they cast lots for them and the lot fell on Matthias; and he was added to the eleven apostles" (Acts 1:15–26).

At the Last Supper Jesus says in his prayer for unity: "Holy Father, protect them in your name that you have given me....While I was with them, I protected them in your name....I guarded them, and not one of them was lost except the one destined to be lost..." (John 17:11–12).

When bishops act in the name of the Lord, they are successors of the apostles. Jesus continues to pray for them: "I am not asking you to take them out of the world, but I ask you to protect them from the evil one" (John 17:15).

There are times when the successors of the apostles betray Jesus as Judas did. "But see, the one who betrays me is with me, and his hand is on the table. For the Son of Man is going as it has been determined, but woe to that one by whom he is betrayed!" (Luke 22:21). We are not to follow them.

And just as Jesus said that anyone who scandalized one of these little ones should have a millstone put around his neck and be thrown in the depths of the sea, so in Mark he says at the Last Supper: "For the Son of Man goes as it is written of him, but woe to that one by whom the Son of Man is betrayed! It would have been better for that one not to have been born" (Mark 14:21).

St. Augustine in his treatise *On Shepherds* says:

> The wicked shepherds do not spare the sheep. It is not enough that they neglect those who are ill and weak, those that go astray and are lost. They even try, insofar as it is in their power, to kill the strong and the healthy. Yet such sheep live. Yes, by God's mercy they live. As for the wicked shepherds themselves, they kill the sheep. How do they kill them, you ask? By their wicked lives and by giving bad example...even the strong sheep, if he turns his eyes from the Lord's laws and looks at demands set over him, notices that his shepherd is living wickedly and begins to say in his heart: if my pas-

tor lives that way, why should I not live like him? The wicked shepherd kills the strong sheep.[8]

Matthew's Gospel says it this way:

[A]nd while they were eating, he said, "Truly I tell you, one of you will betray me." And they became greatly distressed and began to say to him one after another, "Surely not I, Lord?" He answered, "The one who has dipped his hand into the bowl with me will betray me. The Son of Man goes as it is written of him, but woe to that one by whom the Son of Man is betrayed! It would have been better for that one not to have been born." Judas, who betrayed him, said: "Surely not I, Rabbi?" He replied, "You have said so." (Matt 26:21–25)

The *Catechism* states: "[Bishops] sanctify the Church by their example, not domineering over those in charge but being examples to the flock. Thus together with the flock entrusted to them they may attain eternal life."[9] So the successors of the apostles are not important because they wear fancy clothes or have a rather strange hat called a miter and a cross around their neck. They are important to the degree that they preach the gospel to us and faithfully administer the sacraments. The degree to which they act like Judas is the degree to which their example is not to be followed and in these circumstances they are not to be obeyed.

The difference between apostles and medieval princes is clear. A medieval prince had the power to order his people to do things, some of which were right and some of which were wrong. Not to obey the prince, even when he ordered his subjects to do something wrong, would either land his subject in prison or have him exiled outside the prince's territorial domain. Not to follow someone acting as a successor of Judas will land you closer to the Lord, not farther away.

This distinction between times when bishops act as successors of the apostles and when they act as successors of Judas is one of the most important internal limits on the use of their pastoral office. It is scripturally based. They are not princes, and obedience to them as princes is not obedience to the gospel. Many today advocate checks and balances on episcopal power by instituting such natural-law practices as due process, trial by jury, and arbitration procedures. These reforms will tilt most bishops away from arbitrary behavior. As good as these suggestions are, it seems to me that our scripturally based distinction does more to indicate bishops are under the law and not above it.

It is also important to remember that in the long history of the church, Jesus' cleansing of the Temple (John 2:13–22), mentioned earlier in this chapter, is often invoked by the fathers and medieval saints as an illustration of Jesus cleansing his church. Franciscan writers use it as an example of his driving corruption out of the church of their time, especially the sin of simony. A beautiful example is the scene powerfully depicted by Giotto di Bondone for the Scrovegni Chapel in Padua.

6. It is also important to remember that there is only one Good Shepherd and that is Jesus.

No matter how holy bishops or pastors may be, they are not the Good Shepherd and it is wrong to treat them as if they were. They are helpers of the Good Shepherd. In a sacramental way, they share through ordination a mediating/ instrumental role in the Good Shepherd's saving acts. St. Augustine says it this way: "Good shepherds are one in the one Good Shepherd. They form a unity. If only they feed the sheep, Christ is feeding the sheep. Christ, Himself, is the Shepherd when they act as shepherds. Feed them, He says, because His voice is their voice and His love is their love."[10]

But they are not Jesus and they are not the Good Shepherd, and we should not treat them that way. They are, however, holy in the sense that they are set apart for a sacred ministry and share as pastoral vicars or stand-ins for Jesus. That is why they are called to a higher standard.

On a personal note I must tell you how often, when I stand at the altar just before the consecration, I say what Peter said to Jesus on the shore of Lake Tiberias after the miraculous catch of fishes: "Go away from me, Lord, for I am a sinful man!" (Luke 5:8).

7. God does not always speak through theophanies.

Balaam, an Old Testament prophet who was not an Israelite, was on a mission for a king who was at war with Israel (Num 22:28–32). If you recall, the Lord talked to Balaam through his donkey. It took him a little time to figure that out.

"Then the LORD opened the eyes of Balaam, and he saw the angel of the LORD standing in the road, with his drawn sword in his hand; and he bowed down, falling on his face" (Num 22:31). This is a crucial point: Do you have sense enough to listen when the Lord speaks to you in this way?

I like to remind my boys and girls here at Boys Town that if God can speak through Balaam's donkey, then he can speak through Val J. Peter. Not too often, but at least sometimes. And it is important for me to remember that, because he sent me to preach the gospel and not to be ashamed of it.

56

8. There is a phrase used from ancient times down to our own day, namely, that the priest is an "alter Christus."

In one sense it is correct to say that a priest is another Christ; but our culture finds this sense to be so obscure and so difficult to grasp that, in my opinion, it should be set aside for a time and stricken from the vocabulary of our culture.[11] It can be brought back when the culture changes. Why? Because it will inevitably lead to more misunderstanding than understanding. Why? Because it will in our age make it more difficult to distinguish between the pope as successor of Peter and the pope as Simon. And more difficult to distinguish between a bishop as successor of the apostles and as successor of Judas.

All these distinctions clearly point to the fact that our expectations about those in authority should be realistic and appropriate to the age. To expect church authority to live the gospel and strive for holiness is right and proper. Yet to expect church authority to be without sin is unrealistic. And then again, to allow them to continue in serious sin is unholy. It is unrealistic to think that God cannot speak through them, as he really does.

Hans Urs von Balthasar puts it this way: "According to Christ, Himself, the Church which He founded is only credible in the saints, and those who try to make the love of Christ the basis of everything. It is they who reveal what the Church really is in its authentic state, while sinners who do not seriously believe in God's love only obscure it."[12]

9. There is a big difference between secular authority and the authority the Lord assigned to his church.

Our children need to learn this. If we love the Lord, we will listen to him in faith. "Speak, LORD, for your servant is listening"(1 Sam 3:9) is an attitude of every true prophet,

57

every true missionary, and every true follower of the Lord. And we will listen when the church speaks.

The degree to which a secular leader acts on behalf of the common good of the people is the degree to which he fulfills the role that the Lord has called him to. But we do not owe the secular leader obedience except when the law calls for it. We must obey the just laws of government. But the American democracy is a "government of laws, not men."

This is not the place to enter the debate regarding Paul's insistence that "whoever resists authority resists what God has appointed" (Rom 13:2) and Peter being remembered as saying, "We must obey God rather than any human authority" (Acts 5:29).

The government is not an instrument of salvation, but rather the church is. The Bible is the word of God, whereas the Constitution of the United States is the word of very wise men.

There are times, and they may be frequent or rare depending upon the circumstances, when we need to disobey secular authority, but there are never times when we need to disobey God's laws because that would be rebellion against the Lord himself. De Lubac points out the true inner law of the church is the Holy Spirit while some canons of the church are mere penal law.[13]

10. There is a difference between the gospel and good news.

Yes, good news is the meaning of the Greek word translated into English as *gospel*. The gospel is good news, but not all good news is the gospel. When I hear that Notre Dame wins a football game I say that is good news, but it is not the Gospel. When I hear that one of my Boys Town seniors has won a four-year scholarship to college, that is good news, but it is not the gospel.

Some ministers, priests, and bishops who preach in America have succumbed to the environmental conditioning of our culture that does not believe we should be called sinners. ("Who gives you the right to make me feel guilty?") It is a "feel-good" religion that is preached, a religion often based on recovery from illness and on learning from our mistakes. This is not the preaching of the gospel. It may illustrate what Dietrich Bonhoeffer called "cheap grace" to preach that we have a Redeemer and Savior who wants us to concentrate not on his forgiving our sins and calling us to glory, but on our need for self-esteem and self-affirmation. So there is a kind of confusion that happens in our land when a priest or bishop or professor or minister is tempted to sugarcoat the gospel and to say he has the good news of the gospel when he does not.

Since Vatican II at times some church leaders have said things that have misled or confused the faithful in the area of personal morality. St. Paul reminds us often of false teachers: "[I]f anyone proclaims to you a gospel contrary to what you have received, let that one be accursed!" (Gal 1:9). The Old Testament is filled with examples of false prophets who told people "the news is good," when the opposite was true. Remember Jeremiah the prophet surrounded by false prophets who proclaimed the message of peace. The people wanted to hear that message and they did not want to hear Jeremiah's call to repentance. The message of peace seemed like good news to the people at the time. But those prophets of good news were false prophets; their message was a false message. Jerusalem was destroyed and the people were led into captivity (Jer 8:10–12).

It sounds like good news when you are told that you should put yourself first. If you do, your examination of conscience will be something like this: "Was I good to myself today? Did I do enough for me? Did I forgive me? Did I grow in self-esteem?" That might sound like good news, but it is not the gospel. "[W]hoever does not take up the cross and follow me is not worthy of me" (Matt 10:38).

Living a lifestyle that expounds countercultural values and a way of life is not easy. It is reminiscent of Celsus, the second-century writer who, as a bitter pagan, around AD 178 wrote a hate-filled attack on Christians and their way of life. What he ridiculed most was how the Christian faith appealed to the common people: the poor, the slave, the destitute, the outcast. The great church father Origen quotes Celsus's description of the Christian point of view as follows: "Let no cultured person draw near, none wise, none sensible, for all that kind of thing we count evil. But if any man is ignorant, if any is wanting in sense and culture, if any is a fool, let him come boldly."[14] With contempt he wrote of Christians: "We see them in their own houses, wool dressers, cobblers, and fullers, the most uneducated and vulgar persons."[15] He said Christians were "like a swarm of bats…or ants creeping out of their anthills…or frogs holding a symposium in a swamp…or worms in convention in a corner of the mud."[16]

11. The traditional teaching of the church is that the Lord places bishops and pastors over us in two ways, either through his positive will or through his permissive will.

Through his positive will he puts people in authority over us who are by and large good role models, who preach the gospel "in season and out…when convenient and when inconvenient." Even these people have faults because they are mere mortals and they are in need of salvation through Jesus Christ as much as we are. They cling to the Lord and his saving power and it is a joy to have them sharing in God's authority over us, his people.

Through his permissive will God also allows people to exercise authority over us who act like Simon and not like Peter, who act like Judas and not like the other apostles. These overseers are pastors or bishops or administrators who have crossed the line, violating the minimal standards of decency. If God allowed Judas to be an apostle who would betray the Lord, why should we be surprised if the Lord allows someone over us for a time who betrays him in a similar fashion.

The distinction between bishops acting like successors of the apostles and bishops acting like successors of Judas is a critical one for reform and renewal in the church. Church historians have often pointed out times when secular theories of government were incorporated into canon law and theology. For example, when pagan Rome moved away from democracy to monarchy in the time of Augustus and succeeding emperors, the notion of the divine right of kings grew strong and waxed eloquent, as evidenced by imperial coinage. On the emperor Hadrian's coins, Jupiter confers power on him. And this secular innovation became confused with the biblical keys of St. Peter.

12. Legitimate authority in the church ought to be praised only when it acts fairly and justly.

St. Augustine says something quite beautiful about this. It is a personal comment about himself:

> I must clearly distinguish between two aspects of the role the Lord has given me, a role that demands a rigorous accountability, a role based on the Lord's greatness rather than on my own merit. The first aspect is that I am a Christian. The second, that I am a leader. I am a Christian for my own sake,

whereas I am a leader for your sake. The fact that I am a Christian is to my own advantage. But I am a leader for your advantage. Many people come to God as Christians, but not as leaders. Perhaps they travel by an easier road and are less hindered since they bear a lighter burden. We need to pray for those whom God has appointed over us.[17]

The fact that a pastor or bishop or pope acts in accord with the law, exercising legitimate authority, does not make his action morally right. Is there any historical precedent for worrying about this? Yes, every Jew in Nazi Germany sent to their death in a concentration camp was sent legally, in accord with the law. In Stalin's time, officials sending Soviet citizens to the Gulag did so legally, following all the prescriptions of the law. So, too, bishops can follow the prescribed procedures of canon law and misuse their authority, acting unjustly.

13. Failure to exercise legitimate authority when called for is as great a problem as exercising authority unfairly and unjustly.

Many parents are afraid to discipline their children due to a culture of recrimination. Many teachers are reluctant to discipline their students due to a culture of laissez-faire. Many supervisors will not lead decisively out of fear of micromanaging. Many bishops are restrained from bringing purification and reform to their dioceses out of a need to be "pastoral," namely, out of lack of courage and immoderate need to be liked.

Courage and wisdom are in short supply and always have been. Humans aspire to what is noble, but often do what is expedient.

THE EXAMPLE OF LEADERS

How many leaders when faced with situations that needed to be rectified simply had no courage to act? John F. Kennedy's *Profiles in Courage* and Dietrich Bonhoeffer's *The Cost of Discipleship* offer good examples of those who had the courage to act.

It takes time and practice to make these distinctions part of our spiritual lives. Consider the following examples.

1. Can you imagine in the Catholic Church of America a situation where bishops routinely begin asking themselves, both privately and publicly: Am I acting as a successor of the apostles or as a successor of Judas? They may do so privately, but we have never heard it publicly.

   The day that becomes part of their examination of conscience (not just for a few) is the day when noble reform will begin to advance and take a giant step forward. As a result, that will be the day when priests and religious may begin more frequently to ask themselves: Am I a follower of the Good Shepherd or partly a wolf pretending to be a shepherd? Through this role modeling, laymen and laywomen will be much more likely to ask themselves: Am I a doer of the word or only a hearer? Am I ashamed of the gospel or do I embrace the gospel?

2. Remember October 16, 1978, when the new successor of St. Peter, John Paul II, appeared on the balcony of St. Peter's and said, "Do not be afraid to welcome Christ and accept His authority."[18] He did not say: "Welcome me and accept my authority." What good role modeling.

And twenty-five years later on October 16, 2003, Pope John Paul said, "Today, dear brothers and sisters, I am happy to share with you an experience that has extended to a quarter of a century. Every day the same dialogue between Jesus and Peter takes place within my heart....Even though He is aware of my human fragility, God encourages me to respond with faith like Peter."[19]

How wonderful it was to see this successor of Peter tell people that, deep down in his own soul, he realized that to be a "perfect pope" or "perfect successor of St. Peter" does not mean either, as a conservative, keeping all the rules and protocols of our denomination exactly and precisely, nor does it mean, as a progressive, being perfectly attuned to working for justice, prophetically calling for environmental reforms and the perfect embrace of all other liberal causes of the day. Rather, it means answering Jesus' question: "Peter, do you love me?"

How touching it was to read in Pope John Paul's spiritual testament released on April 7, 2005, after his death, the following: "As for the funeral, I repeat the same dispositions as were given by the Holy Father Paul VI." (Here is a note in the margin: "burial in the bare earth, not in a sarcophagus.")[20]

And then he adds: "For with the Lord is mercy and with Him is plenteous redemption."

3. How marvelous it was that at the election of Benedict XVI the pilgrims gathered in St. Peter's Square refrained from the proclaiming, "You are the greatest," as some athletes and performers tend to desire from the crowds, but they simply rejoiced in God's mercy and his faithfulness to us. Pope John XXIII, recalling

the moment the cardinals elected him as Peter's successor, said, "How could I not tremble, humanly speaking....It was necessary to rely on divine mercy."[21]

The coat of arms of Joseph Cardinal Ratzinger, when he was made archbishop of Munich, embodies two symbols: a scalloped shell which is the emblem of those going on pilgrimage for we have here no lasting city (Heb 13:14) and a bear. What about the bear?

The bear comes from a legend about the first bishop of Munich, St. Korbinian, who once, when traveling to Rome, found that a bear attacked the horse carrying his luggage. The good saint said that as a result of killing his horse, the bear had to carry his luggage to Rome.

In 1997, Joseph Ratzinger wrote:

Isn't Korbinian's bear compelled against his will to carry the Saint's pack a picture of my own life? The legend says that Korbinian set the bear free once he reached Rome. It doesn't tell us whether the animal went to the Abruzzi Mountains or returned to the Alps. Meanwhile, I have carried my pack to Rome and wander for some time now through the streets of the Eternal City. When release will come I cannot know. What I do know is that I am God's pack animal, and as such close to Him.[22]

It reminds me of Balaam's donkey. And now Benedict XVI has to stay in Rome and carry that luggage all the way to eternal life.

Let us strive to make authority in the church so honorable, so scripture based, and so attractive that more and more Catholics will be inclined to listen appreciatively, to speak creatively, and to work together humbly.

It will be wonderful when we can so internalize distinctions such as these that our spiritual lives are enriched. With sextants to shoot the stars, ancient mariners guided their ships to reach homeport. Our ideals are like the stars. We will never reach them. But we use them to arrive at our homeport, namely, heaven. High ideals and low expectations are the daily lot of pilgrims on their way to the promised land.

Chapter 4

SELECTIVE OPENNESS

The second secular challenge is uncritical openness. Many praise the openness of postmodern society as compared with the intolerance of days gone by, and yet the culture we live in promotes uncritical openness. Popular culture often looks with disdain and disapproval on the practice of discernment of spirits, which holds there are certain things we should not be open to. A person who is not open to everything is said to be petty and small and closeminded. Larger society tends to praise diversity uncritically and those who oppose it are said to be lacking in compassion and care. They are not considered "cool" but "old-fashioned" and "out-of-date."

IMPLICATIONS OF
UNCRITICAL OPENNESS

"To be cool" (a popular expression among many young people in this generation) is to be *forward-looking*. And forward-looking people are open to experiencing all things. A question for everyone committed to growing spiritually and to purification of the church is this: Should we be free to experience everything? In this chapter the elements of indiscriminate openness and how to deal with this secular challenge will be considered.

This question is most clearly enunciated in the area of sexuality. The mantra repeated over and over again among those in junior or senior high today is that you should "be open to explore your own sexuality." Is sexuality simply love energy as some suggest or is it something more ambiguous? Does it need to flow freely without hindrance or should everyone's vehicle have a brake as well as a gas pedal? Do you only require good self-esteem and communication skills to guide you through the openness? Does marriage need to be polymorphous? Do religious sisters, brothers, and priests need to be "open to the third way"? ("The third way" is an expression used to describe some middle ground between marriage and celibacy.) Do preadolescents need to be open to explore their sexuality and do adolescents need to be open to explore the gay lifestyle if the energy flows that way on any given day? What about drugs?

The proponents of indiscriminate or uncritical openness are fond of telling stories of people raised in rigid, ultraconservative religious sects and then going to the opposite extreme when given the opportunity. The conversation often sounds something like this: *Don't be a prude. Be open. Embrace diversity.* These proponents revel in novels written about young women raised in such a strict, puritanical society that they become chief actors in *Desperate Housewives.*

Proponents of indiscriminate openness embrace Freud's belief that neuroses tend to develop in people whose superego is too rigid, too severe, and too controlling. They like the way Freud saw himself as the new Moses, whose destiny was to abolish both the Law on Mt. Sinai and the Law Giver. In addition, there is the perennial male adolescent fantasy that somewhere out there is a world without sexual restraints, if only we could find it.

On the other hand, those who question indiscriminate openness and who promote a more selective approach like to tell the story of William Coulson, PhD.[1] Years ago he was a disciple of the famous Carl Rogers and a copractitioner of his nondirective therapy.

AN EXAMPLE TO CONSIDER

At the University of Wisconsin Carl Rogers had experienced repeated success with his unconditional positive regard toward sick patients by helping them open up to their potential. This was at the beginning of what is today known as the human-potential movement.

Dr. Rogers was seen by his colleagues as an upright moral person. He was thought to hold firmly to the Ten Commandments as traditionally understood. He mistakenly assumed that his patients would have such a well-formed conscience that, when they opened themselves to their potential, they would not lie, cheat, steal, or commit adultery.

The National Institute of Mental Health was quite pleased with his work in Wisconsin. He wanted to extend his research to healthy people. If sick people could profit from his nondirective therapy by opening themselves up to their potential, what about well people? He started to believe that everyone, no matter how healthy, could profit from nondirective counseling. He and his fellow psychologists moved to Southern California where they looked for a group of healthy persons with whom to conduct this experiment of encounter groups and sensitivity-training sessions.[2]

This experiment proved to be a disaster for many reasons. The participants had no mentors to warn them about the excesses of what they were about to experience. The goal was to help them "achieve their own potential." During the process, the participants were indiscriminately encouraged to go against what they were trained to be, to call it "phoniness" (a buzzword of the times), and to say what was deepest within them. Part of what is deepest within each human being is our sexual side. In simple terms, libido was released. Many of the groups did not really know or comprehend what was happening. They had no one to warn them they were being sold a mess of pottage. Indiscriminate energy by its nature dissipates quickly and what remains is emptiness. It ruined lives.

Some of Dr. Rogers's counselors began teaching their participants to play sexual games in therapy sessions. This was a potential that participants had not focused on before, and doing so now led to disastrous results. Indiscriminate openness led to grave harm.

"Rogers didn't get people involved in sex games, but he couldn't prevent his followers from doing it...we didn't have a doctrine of evil....When we implied to people that they could trust their impulses, they also understood us to mean that they could trust their evil impulses, that they weren't really evil. But they were really evil."[3]

In Dr. Coulson's words: "We overcame their traditions. We overcame their faith."[4] All of this was happening within a context of the Catholic Church's Second Vatican Council—opening the windows as Blessed Pope John XXIII put it to let some fresh air in. And although most everyone today agrees that the life of many religious was in those days excessively rigid, excessively narrow, and excessively controlled, Carl Rogers's solution was clearly the wrong one.

The church in America was moving out of its childhood into its early adolescence, and the strong cultural currents of freedom from restraints were at work in helping the participants achieve their potential. What is the inner dynamic at work here in this kind of indiscriminate or uncritical openness?

THE DYNAMICS OF UNCRITICAL OPENNESS

First come *thoughts* something along the lines of "I just realized that I have been duped all my life by a puritanical church that through the centuries has said over and over again that sex is bad and forbidden. My potential has been completely frustrated; it was blocked and buried deep within me. I need to experience freedom from my past."

Feelings follow: Outrage that I have been deprived of exploring my sexuality by a church that has been repressing my feelings and sexual urges, which the popular media and culture strongly suggest. Feelings of anger and self-loathing arise as I become cynical in rejecting my past.

Next comes *behavior* in accord with my new thoughts and feelings. I need now to explore my sexuality in areas I was forbidden to explore before and this time there can be no limits, provided it is open, caring, and does not hurt anyone. The popular, secular culture seems to applaud this approach.

Further Examples

British journalist Sally Feldman, writing about why she is "glad my daughter had underage sex," speaks of her daughter and her friends: "Once they began to be sexually active, they used to march each other down to the local family planning clinic. Anyone who dared to try unprotected sex would be dealt with severely by the girls. They all experimented with sex early, had boyfriends who were lovers and others were friends and are turning into delightfully well-balanced young women."[5]

A more tragic example of this indiscriminate openness is the 2002 book, *Harmful to Minors: The Perils of Protecting Children from Sex*, by Judith Levine.[6] She writes effusively about a Dutch law that gives adults freedom to have sexual relations with children as young as twelve, provided it is consensual. Think of the poor children who are harmed by such toxic advice. This is classic indiscriminate openness.

How we might profit from reading Benedict XVI's *Deus Caritas Est:* "True, eros tends to rise 'in ecstasy' towards the Divine, to lead us beyond ourselves; yet for this very reason it calls for a path of ascent, renunciation, purification and healing" (n. 5).

Recently, Dr. Lawrence Cunningham, professor of theology at Notre Dame in South Bend, Indiana, told an interesting story regarding this matter at a meeting of Foundations and Donors Interested in Catholic Activities, Inc. (FADICA):

> Thomas Merton fell in love with this nurse. And, of course, being Merton he writes about it incessantly…a 53-year-old man in love with a young woman but committed to monastic life.…
>
> When did this happen? This happened post-Vatican II. It was kind of a crazy time, all kinds of things changing. I talked once to a very good friend of Thomas Merton, Ping Ferry, an old left-winger from the West Coast. He died a few years ago. And he told me that when Merton was going

through this experience, Ferry had a long talk with Thomas Merton in Louisville and Merton said (you could kind of hear the rationalization) "Well, maybe I will just quietly leave the monastery."

And Ping said to him, "Quietly leave? Probably the best-known monk in the history of the Catholic Church with 56 books and 5,000 articles is going to kind of quietly leave? I don't think so."

So it was a crazy moment. He overcame it and he remained faithful. I think that is the other important thing to remember.[7]

A very different story is told by Dorothy Day in her autobiography *The Long Loneliness*.[8] She writes about how she was baptized as a baby, but by her teen years her interest in religion had faded. She joined the Socialist Party. All the bright people did in those days. She became interested in all sorts of what she called left-wing causes. She had a free and easy sex life. She spent time with poets and playwrights in Greenwich Village. She got pregnant living with an atheist biologist and was happy to have a baby by him. And yet, for some reason or other, something stirred within her to have the baby baptized. She knew her lover would put his foot down, but she was determined to have the baby baptized. "I knew that I was not going to have her aimlessly floundering through many years as I had done, doubting and hesitating, undisciplined and amoral."[9]

What about her years dedicated to Marxism? "If I could have felt that Communism was the answer to my desire for a cause, a motive, a way to live in, I would have remained as I was. But I felt that only faith in Christ could give the answer. The Sermon on the Mount answered all the questions as to how to love God and one's neighbor."[10]

She surrendered herself to God and became a dedicated Catholic. She puts it this way:

> No human creature could receive or contain so vast a flood of love and joy as I often felt after the birth of my child. With this came the need to worship, to adore. I had many say that they had wanted to worship God in their own way and did not need a Church in which to praise God, nor a body of people with whom to associate themselves. But I did not agree to this. My very experience as a radical, my whole makeup, led me to want to associate myself with others, with the masses, in loving and praising God.[11]

Dorothy Day saw the allegiance of millions of Christians to the church over the centuries as a powerful motivating force.

> She [the Catholic Church] had come through the centuries since the time of Peter, and far from being dead, she claimed and held the allegiance of the masses of people in all the cities where I had lived. They poured in and out of her doors on Sundays and Holy Days, for novenas and missions. What if they were compelled to come in by the law of the Church, which said they were guilty of mortal sin if they did not go to Mass every Sunday? They obeyed that law. They were given a chance to show their preference. They accepted the Church. It may have been an unthinking, unquestioning faith, and yet the chance certainly came again and again, do I prefer the "Church" to my

own will, even if it was only the small matter of sitting at home on a Sunday morning with the papers? And the choice was the Church.[12]

What about being duped by the church's narrow-minded view of things?

I was just as much against capitalism and imperialism as ever, and here I was going over to the opposition...but I wanted to be poor, chaste, and obedient. I wanted to die in order to live, to put off the old me and put on Christ. I loved, in other words, and like all women in love, I wanted to be united to my love....I loved the Church for Christ, Himself. Not for itself because it was so often a scandal to me....With all the knowledge I have gained these twenty-one years I have been a Catholic, I could write many a story of priests who are poor, chaste and obedient, who gave their lives daily for their fellows, but I am writing of how I felt at the time of my baptism.[13]

THE PROBLEMS WITH EXTREME POSITIONS

Just as puritanism is an extreme and leads to many problems, so indiscriminate or uncritical openness leads to great unhappiness. Why? Because both are unbalanced. A successful and happy life is a delicate balance between two extremes: too much openness and too little openness, too much sensitivity and too little sensitivity, too much compassion and too little compassion, too much religion and too little religion, too much restraint and too little restraint.

In evolutionary theory, indiscriminate openness is described as an unsuccessful adaptation to the environment. In the long run it is going to make one's life more difficult, not easier. It is going to make one's life more frustrated, not less frustrated. It often makes one so angry at a church preaching fidelity, chastity, and sacrifice and some priests and bishops seemingly doing the opposite that one can become angry at the very core and becomes an angry person. In other words, anger begins to control one's life. To embrace wholeheartedly a permissive, overeroticized lifestyle brings worse troubles.

It helps to remember that our secular culture roundly rejects what we have been taught in the past, namely, premarital chastity and fidelity in marriage. One is often made to feel that the church has lied to me all these years. I am made to feel ashamed of my past, troubled by my present, and I will only have a happy future if I rebel against the moral restraints that were imposed upon me.

These are new thoughts and they are powerful. Why? Because the people telling us these things seem popular, successful, and influential. They are saying that we have been duped, tricked, and lied to by a church that is "old-fashioned" and way behind the times. These thoughts put a doubt in our mind and confuse people about traditional teaching on sexuality.

Then there are feelings of missing out on the excitement of life, missing out on opportunities for fun and friendship, missing out on what the in-group is enjoying. Also, there are feelings of anger and resentment preparing the neophyte to take the first steps toward indiscriminate openness. What if we have been duped? So you start to poke fun at what you believed before. You start to laugh at people who believe what you used to believe. You start to heap scorn on those who try to reason with you and you begin to have a feeling of solidarity with your culture.

Finally, you start engaging in behaviors you never in the past thought you would engage in. Indiscriminate and permissive sexual activity of many kinds (as long as it is mutual), how can it be wrong if it feels so good and no one is hurt? Experimentation with drugs is part of growing up.

Once the behaviors start to occur they reinforce the feelings of anger against the past, rejection of those who chastise you, and defiance of traditional authority.

Our postmodern culture has far fewer checks or restraints on fear of missing out than in the past. This culture attempts to banish guilt and shame and makes us more vulnerable. It is a very powerful force, more powerful than most of us realize. It takes away many former taboos that were vital for human flourishing in a life-enhancing society.

CONSEQUENCES OF REMOVING INHIBITIONS

Pornography is a good example. In times past, society was structured in such a way that access to pornography was limited through a series of guilt-producing inhibitions. The environment was not favorable to pornography. Even an oppositional/defiant person had to deal with these inhibitions. In other words, in order to gain access to pornography in the past, a person usually would hide their identity (put on a disguise: a trench coat, hat, and dark glasses), drive circuitously to a seedy part of town to find a peep show, making sure nobody saw you enter or exit.

These inhibitions have been removed by our computer-filled environment. There is no need to sneak around anymore, for all one has to do is to turn on a computer in the privacy of your home, office, or public library. It is completely anonymous, so the price of accessing harmful pornography has just gone down, with no societal strictures there to stop a person. The result is that more people are getting addicted to pornography. Like cocaine, it is a quickly addictive experience.

As a person begins to engage in heretofore forbidden behaviors, old-fashioned guilt tends to rise, but it is quickly suppressed. In the twenty-first century there are multilayered environmental currents that help you deny your guilt and shame. The message is repeated over and over again: You need to be free to experience everything. Those whose job it is to call right right and wrong wrong are regularly ridiculed roundly by the media.

SPECIAL PLEADING

Those old enough to have studied logic in times past remember the logical fallacy called "special pleading." It is still a logical fallacy though not much studied. Our old textbooks reminded us that special pleading was most often applied to sexual issues. It amounts to this: We should do away with rules forbidding sexual activity because everyone does it so it can't be wrong.

This logic was never applied, however, to stealing. Even today, though many people steal, we are not in favor of doing away with the laws against stealing. We do not say that stealing can't be wrong because so many people do it. We all know that is rationalization. We really do not want people to steal from us just as others do not want us to steal from them.

So we agree with the commandment: Thou shalt not steal. On occasions when we are tempted to steal we know deep down in our hearts that stealing is wrong. You may argue for a small exception by saying that everybody steals a little bit, so it should not be wrong. But most of us see through this mistake in reasoning and know it is nothing more than a rationalization.

We cannot recognize this rationalization so easily when the issue is sexual activity, whether heterosexual or homosexual. Why do we make an exception for our own sexual acting out when we do not make an exception for our stealing? The answer is clear. Sexuality touches deep human emotions. It symbolizes intimacy and all of us in our heart of hearts deeply want to be loved by someone and truly cherished, and so when the possibility of such sexual exchange arises, we plead an exception for ourselves. Love energy makes towering promises when we are in the grips of it, promises it cannot keep.

One may be tempted to say: "This may be my only chance at love and I'd better grab it while it comes my way because I may never have another chance again. Here is fear of missing out; fear of losing my one chance for love and the only thing stopping me is a set of puritanical rules made by a group of ignorant, celibate males who don't know what they are talking about."

Sexual rationalization appeals to our deepest emotions and is reinforced by the smoldering anger telling us we have been duped by too puritanical a church. We feel like victims.

CONSIDERING THE QUESTION POSED

So the question, *"Am I free to experience everything?"* is really a trick question. Am I free to hit myself with a hammer? Am I free to burn my house down? Am I free to ruin my family? All of these sound profound but they are not helpful at all.

In other words the question, *"Am I free to experience everything?"* is a misleading question because it leads one into a maze with no way out. The answer to the question is yes and no. Am I free to run down the street nude? Yes, but I will be dragged off by a police officer for doing so. So the answer is no.

The road to spiritual and mental health embraces a loud and clear **no** to indiscriminate or uncritical openness, just as the road to spiritual and mental health includes a loud and clear **no** to puritanism. Indiscriminate openness will only make things worse, not better. There are some things I should not do, not even once. They are that harmful. I should not try crystal meth, not even once, just as I should not try cocaine even once. The potential for harm is just too great. The risks far outweigh the rewards.

Spirituality focuses on relationships that promote union with God and others in God. These relationships include limitations on what we can do and cannot do. The scriptures as well as centuries of Christian practice tell us these limitations, namely, divine standards of right and wrong. Can the acceptance of limitations be creative and liberating? Of course it can. For fidelity to our vocation, to God's commandments and to the gospel are the things that bring us true freedom. Freedom to do whatever we like does not bring us fidelity. We become free by being faithful. We do not become faithful by being free.

THE ROLE OF HEROES

Some years ago Rosemary Haughton wrote a quite delightful piece about the need for what she called the "heroic myth" in a world where the "romantic myth" of sexual fulfillment was all too prevalent.[14] It is not, she said, that Romeo and Juliet are woodenheaded but rather that they are not good role models for our children or ourselves today, even though the story is wonderful, heartrending, and inspiring. Tristan and Isolde were lovers driven by passions that they could neither understand nor control. They are not, she thought, role models even though they are a wonderful mythic protest against a loveless world of money, power, and influence.

What we need in our age, according to Haughton, is a rediscovery of the "hero myth." All through history, the pattern of the hero myth is repeated. It is the fairy-tale hero who is sent on a quest and goes willingly when others better equipped and better prepared have no interest or have failed. The mission of the hero is to save the people from dragons and ogres of all sorts. The mission is to heal the king by fetching the water of life, or finding the bird of happiness, or throwing the golden ring into the great fire. The meaning is always the same and, although heroes are in great demand, they are always in short supply.

Haughton rightly says, "The hero is not necessarily a great leader, perhaps of a revolution, but simply one who realizes the human calling, which is to go out and discover the future, symbolically to find the water of life, rescue the princess and kill the dragon."[15]

It is the story of Abraham and Sarah going out in obedience to make a future for a new people. And such an unlikely pair they seemed to be at the start. It is the story of

Moses who follows the Lord's command to go on a mission vital for his people in need to be set free. It is the story of David going out to meet Goliath in a desperate state of unpreparedness. It is Samson, Judith, Esther, Isaiah, Ezekiel, and so many more. It is "one sent by God whose name was John." And it is finally the one born at Bethlehem and raised in Galilee of whom it was said: "What good can come from Galilee?"

Written almost twenty-five years ago, Haughton's comments are prophetic: "Ours are circumstances in which most of the traditional social slots for heroes are temporarily discredited. Priests, scientists, explorers, even revolutionaries, like the elder sons in the fairytales, are not adequate to the quest."[16]

The one quality above all that is needed by a hero is fidelity. Odysseus, in Homer's *Odyssey*, must, above all other things, be faithful if he is to return to his beloved Ithaca. He is not free to be unfettered when experiencing what the Sirens have to offer. Aeneas must be faithful to the quest (*"fatum"*) if he is to found a new people. Parsifal must be faithful to the quest of searching for the Holy Grail and must even be willing to go against what his mother has taught him. Robert Browning's "Poor Roland" must go to the Dark Tower where his sister has been forcibly taken, and he, too, is in a terrible state of unpreparedness.

Haughton writes again: "Extramarital sex may provide new romantic intensity in a life which has lost meaning, but it simply rules out the quest. To turn aside from the quest, as many would-be heroes do in the tales, in order to explore delicious gardens, taste exquisite meals, wander in elegant castles or enjoy gorgeous maidens, is to show a failure to understand the nature of the quest. A hero who does this is literally a non-starter."[17]

The real hero knows and is constantly reminded by a series of "old women, hermits, talking horses, and other embodiments of ancient wisdom—that fidelity is the first and almost the only condition of the quest."[18]

The hero knows instinctively that all the other things that are offered on the road will be very attractive and exceptionally tempting and yet they are to be resisted.

Thus, in the story of Snow White as told by Wilhelm and Jacob Grimm, "The animals came, too, and cried over Snow White, first an owl, then a raven, last a little dove."[19] These three represent the great religions: classical, Greco-Roman paganism is represented by the owl of Athena; the Nordic religion of the forests by the raven of Woden; and the dove is the Christian symbol of the Holy Spirit. Snow White dreams that one day the king's son will come and he does come and he kisses her and she awakes from sleep and she asks him why he came, and he says "because I could not live without you." This is the Christ figure, the great hero who comes to raise us from the dead because he cannot live without us. When she asks why it took him so long he tells her he had to go through a few little troubles. The troubles of Holy Thursday, Good Friday, and Holy Saturday. The hero is Christ faithful to the very end.

It is the Christ who must be faithful to doing his Father's will if he is to free the sleeping beauty from the grip of death. It is self-discipline that starts us on the road to freedom, doing the will of the Father. Doing whatever I want and being open to every whim and fancy brings only dissipation and wantonness.

If I have a good marriage and decide I need to be open to other sexual encounters, I will lose my good marriage. It is fidelity that brings true freedom and true happiness. If I have a good family and I decide I want to be open to drugs,

I will destroy my family and my happiness. It is acceptance of my limitations that is most creative and most liberating. This is one of the great paradoxes of life itself.

BEING FAITHFUL AND FREE

Bernard Haring wrote a very important three-volume work on moral theology titled *Free and Faithful in Christ.* In my opinion, he had it backwards. One starts with being faithful, not with being free. One does not become faithful by being free; you become free by being faithful. By being faithful to the Lord you open your heart to the gift of the Spirit and the Spirit brings true freedom, namely, the ability to love under any circumstances.

Who is the freest person in the world? The one who is most virtuous. The one who can love under any circumstances. Even when they don't feel like it. Even when the other person is unworthy of your love. St. Paul calls this the gift of the Holy Spirit.

Indiscriminate or uncritical openness is to be rejected for the simple reason that we really have *not* been duped all our lives by a puritanical church. The church's central teaching on sex and sexuality (namely, that sexual expression belongs in a faithful marriage between a man and a woman) has been and still is right on target. This teaching preserves the basic values of fidelity, intimacy, trust, compassion, and respect for men and women. It calls us to something greater than self-absorption, namely, it calls us to be a family, and to be a family is a life of self-donation.

This teaching positions marriage as the place where friendship can best flourish and children can best be nourished. It integrates the essential elements of God's call to each person, which is their vocation, as well as sacrificial self-donation (not self-absorption), and salvation by God (not self-salvation).

CONCLUDING THOUGHTS

Through the ages, there have been gross aberrations such as Jansenism, a very puritanical form of Catholicism from the seventeenth century. In no age does the church's teaching remain in a vacuum; in our times the temptation is egocentrism, namely, putting myself first in embracing a culture of death: abortion, divorce, abuse, neglect of children, adultery, and homosexual activity.

Too much uncritical dissent that is harmful to self and others starts with rejection of the church's central teaching on sexuality. The sweeping claim that we have been duped by a puritanical church is not accurate and seems to be nothing more than an attempt to marginalize all who want to hold us responsible for our own behavior. Let us live lives whereby we are not ashamed of the gospel. Let us follow Paul who tells the Ephesians: "Of this gospel I have become a servant according to the gift of God's grace....Although I am the very least of all the saints, this grace was given to me to bring to the Gentiles the news of the boundless riches of Christ, and to make everyone see what is the plan of the mystery hidden for ages in God...so that *through the church* the wisdom of God in its rich variety might now be made known to the rulers and authorities in the heavenly places" (Eph 3:7–11, emphasis mine).

The church's opponents clap their hands with glee at the horrors that have taken place in our church. And some Catholics leave the church in disgust. Is that the only reasonable response? *No.* This is the church founded by Jesus Christ on the faith of Peter and the apostles. So why not stay and help purify God's holy church? She is in sore distress to the great delight of the devil and his angels. We must again heed the words of Hebrews: "Consider him who endured such hostility against himself from sinners, so that you may not grow weary or lose heart" (Heb 12:3). That was the approach of St. Francis and St. Dominic in their day; it was also the approach of St. Francis de Sales, St. Charles Borromeo, and St. Catherine of Siena.

So the question, *"Am I free to experience everything?"* is a trick question. By discarding indiscriminate openness, one needs to embrace selective openness. What is the criterion of selection? Whatever in accord with the gospels increases our union with God and others in God.

Chapter 5
THE REMEDY FOR CYNICISM

The third secular challenge is cynicism, which is deeply imbedded in our culture. It is pernicious and toxic. In acute cases, its effects can be catastrophic for one's spiritual life. Cynicism is a characteristic of our times. Many are cynical toward politicians, lawyers, used-car salesmen, and even clergy. References to *Leave It to Beaver* are used as a cynical slam about family life.

Much of this is cultural conditioning. One breathes a cynical air that pervades our lives. It corrodes any efforts at church renewal and purification. It negates spirituality. If all you take away from this book is the courage to move beyond cynicism it will all have been worthwhile.

SOME HISTORICAL CONSIDERATIONS

The manufacture of cynicism has become a large industry that started in Nazi Germany in the twentieth century. In 1936–37 Adolf Hitler was consolidating his power in Germany. In his mind, too many Germans were still loyal to the

Catholic Church and that was a problem because he wanted them to embrace Nazism instead.

His propaganda minister, Josef Goebbels, hit upon a great idea: Create among the people deep and abiding cynicism about the Catholic Church. How? By trying priests and religious for gross sexual immorality and thereby shocking people with stories of repulsive behaviors of those who were supposed to be paragons of virtue. Make the whole idea of Catholicism repugnant and create widespread cynicism.

A courageous German work originally written in 1941 has a long section entitled "The So-Called Immorality Trials."[1] The following is an example of what this anonymous author calls a "weapon of primary importance in [Nazism's) attack on the Church."

> The Propaganda Minister, Dr. Goebbels, excelled all others in the propagation of incredible charges against the Church. In a speech relayed by all German wireless stations on May 28th, 1937, his assertions were so sweeping and the style adopted was so vulgar and savoured so much of marketplace oratory that one can only assume that hatred of the Church carried the able Propaganda Minister away, and made him incapable of realizing the disastrous effect of his attacks. This speech, which aroused indignation in all foreign countries, contained the following choice remarks:
>
> "A vast number of Catholic clerics have been tried for sexual crimes....It is not a matter of regrettable individual lapses, but of a general corruption of morals such as the history of civilization has scarcely ever known....No other class of society has ever come to shelter such depravity....

In our civilized world no other class of society has contrived to practice immorality and indulge in filth on a scale resembling that achieved by the German clergy in all its ranks....We cannot possibly impose legal sanctions on unnatural vice and at the same time allow thousands upon thousands of priests and brothers of religious Orders to escape scot-free....A very large number of these priests and religious work in the confessional.... There is no doubt that even the thousands of cases which have come to light represent but a small fraction of the total moral corruption."[2]

On May 18, 1937, Cardinal Mundelein of Chicago addressed more than five hundred of his priests saying of these "Immorality Trials":

Now the present German government is making use of...propaganda against the Catholic Church and is giving out through its crooked minister of propaganda stories of wholesale immorality in religious institutions, in comparison to which the wartime propaganda (of the Allies in World War I) is almost like bedtime stories for children...people outside of the Church and perhaps the lukewarm among our own people, reading these things constantly repeated will come to the conclusion "well they are all alike."

These National Socialist enthusiasts who hate the Catholic Church as a "foreign" institution naturally rejoice in its misfortunes and make as much of the Trials as they can.

Perhaps you will ask how it is that a nation of 6,000,000 intelligent people will submit in fear and servitude to an alien, an Austrian paper-hanger, and a darn poor one at that I am told....

Never before was the Church in Germany as helpless as it is today.[3]

The anonymous author of the 1941 work rightly says:

In using the "Immorality" trials in the Russian fashion as a kind of exhibition, a continuous serial picture, the Nazi authorities had no intention of purifying the Church or national morality. To them they were simply just another means of destroying the Church, a weapon in the fight. The moral indignation expressed by these leaders and by the press of the Party was sheer hypocrisy, and its only aim was to arouse in the public, and especially in the minds of Catholics, a certain horror and disgust at the very sight of priests and Religious, and thus to alienate them from the Church.[4]

Yes the propaganda worked to a considerable degree. Cynicism toward the institutional church was the goal and it became more widespread; not a few abandoned the church and entered the temple of the Nordic gods of Aryan superiority, especially among the young. Many more simply became silent out of fear.

CONTEMPORARY CYNICISM
AND ITS ORIGINS

In our own time we have heard story after story of unfaithful priests and religious harming children and adolescents grievously. Quite apart from the obvious exaggeration and excessive sensationalism, of which there is much, the reality is terrible and gross.

The ground becomes even more fertile for cynicism because our families at home are often not working well either. Our out-of-control children and our out-of-control marriages are breeding grounds for cynicism corroding our spirituality and impacting church renewal. The stories we hear of dioceses going bankrupt and bishops appearing before grand juries do not help.

So let us begin by looking at what cynicism is, how it works, and how it can be neutralized. What is a cynic? A cynic is someone who knows the price of everything and the value of nothing. Cynicism is a combination of disappointment and bitterness.

No one sets out to be a cynic. I know of no one who gets up in the morning and says, "I intend to be disappointed at whatever the media reports about the church today and at the end of the day I will share my bitterness with others." No one watches reality shows and says, "I am watching this to become cynical about love and marriage."

Cynicism is something that happens to us. In fact, we let it happen to us, but so often we do not even know we are letting it happen.

Cynicism is like food poisoning in the family and in the church; it turns your stomach and makes you spiritually ill. Cynicism is like a virus in institutional settings: the workplace, the school, the rectory, and so many other places. It is like winter street salt pitting the surface of your vehicle; it spreads easily to newcomers. A cynic has nothing good to say about anything or anybody, anytime, anywhere, and you don't even have to ask a cynic because he is a self-starter. Cynicism is a fungus hurting families. It is like a mold that starts to cover everything and make it unattractive and unusable.

TWO BASIC ELEMENTS OF CYNICISM

It is important to consider what be may described as the two basic elements of cynicism: *trigger mechanisms* and *setting events*.

The idea of a trigger is easy to understand. A trigger is any circumstance or event that is present right before the onset of inappropriate behavior, such as cynicism. Something is said or done by an individual that evokes a strong cynical reaction from others.

The second item that helps explain cynicism is the idea of setting events. Setting events refer to the ecology or setting in which the cynicism occurs. For example, the setting events of the family with an alcoholic father is the ecology of dysfunctionality, the environment of day-to-day squabbling between mom and dad, due to dad's drinking, the all-pervading sense of unhappiness, gloom, and loss of hope. Try as she might, mom's energies are consumed by dad's alcoholism and her son feels like an outsider.

Here is a school example. Let us say you are a first-grade teacher with a little boy who, when you gave the first assignment of the morning (and it was a tough one), began pouting and became uncooperative. Let us say the setting event is the fact that once again today he did not have any breakfast and came to school hungry and distracted. These are common setting events for a fair number of cynical behaviors of school children.

Let us now take one by one the examples of cynicism in the church and in families and see how we can neutralize them and grow spiritually. These two are intertwined and the cynicism in one tends to migrate to the others as well. Two things, *setting events* and *triggers*, need to be considered.

Cynicism in the Church

Here is a typical pattern of *setting events* in our day. For months and months, the scandalous sexual abuse by clerics was reported regularly in the media. The widespread negligence of certain bishops to stop the crimes by not reporting them and covering them up was also in the media spotlight. Bishops were portrayed as protecting each other like self-serving fraternity brothers. People see a guild mentality at work here: Physicians tend not to report on fellow members of their guild, and the same is true of lawyers and bishops. In the church, there was a widespread atmosphere of fear and intimidation, with laity being made to feel guilty for their feelings of anger and outrage. Church lawyers were speaking for bishops as if the church were like a major business corporation. Bishops were not acting like successors of the apostles, but like successors of Judas.

Philip Jenkins in *The New Anti-Catholicism* makes the setting events strikingly clear:

> Long-standing media hostility to the Catholic Church was expressed in singularly frank terms in 2002, during what was commonly (and misleadingly) called the nation's "pedophile priest" crisis. Even reputable news outlets presented a picture of a

Catholic priesthood heavily infiltrated by perverts and child molesters, whose activities were treated so mildly by their superiors that the bishops themselves were virtually accomplices. This awful picture gave the opportunity for the widespread public expression of grotesquely anti-Catholic and anti-clerical sentiments and the revival of every ancient stereotype—even the sale of indulgences.[5]

This context was fertile ground for growing a new crop of cynics.

Some recent and widely reported instances of lack of credibility by church leaders in the media became *common triggers,* namely, events fostering the onset or growth spurts of widespread cynicism due to manifest lack of honesty and discontent with leadership that failed miserably.

As a result of these setting events and common triggers, there is a slow building up of angry, cynical attitudes year after year on the part of very many dedicated and committed Catholic faithful. Frustration with the institutional church increases, and this adversely affects the morale of clergy, religious, and laity. Some even start to believe that spirituality without the church is the way to go. So widespread is this cynicism that evangelical preachers are now saying the age of institutional Christianity is over. We should all leave the churches and practice private spirituality. Shall we light a candle or curse the darkness? Shall we be overcome by evil or, following Paul's advice, should we "overcome evil by doing good"? Paul writes to the Ephesians: "[T]ake up the whole armor of God, so that you may be able to withstand on that evil day....Stand therefore and fasten the belt of truth around your waist, and put on the breastplate of righteousness....[T]ake the shield of faith, with which you will be able to quench all the flaming arrows of the evil one. Take the helmet of salvation, and the sword of the Spirit, which is the word of God" (Eph 6:13–17).

How are we to fight this corrosive cynicism? By learning cynicism reduction and practicing constructive self-restraint.

Practicing constructive self-restraint involves becoming proficient in noncynical responses to trigger mechanisms. It is a matter of practice, practice, practice. Constructive self-restraint not only stops cynical responses, but it moves you to positive action. In many cases, constructive self-restraint involves pointing out the difference between honest reporting and get-even prejudice.

Some Steps to Consider

So constructive self-restraint also means learning about the history of anti-Catholic prejudice. A good place to start is Philip Jenkins's *The New Anti-Catholicism*. Constructive self-restraint also means responding to the cynical comments of fellow workers: "How can you remain a Catholic with such a poor leader as a bishop?" Perhaps the response should be something like "Why would I leave the family founded by Jesus on the faith of the apostles. Stand aside and just watch us clean up our act." Constructive self-restraint means extending a helping hand to discouraged Catholics by sharing your courage with them. It also means helping your pastor and bishop stand up and be counted on the side of the Lord.

The more instances you have of success in responding constructively to trigger mechanisms, the better you begin to feel about yourself. And the better you begin to feel about yourself, the more you are motivated to join with others to fix what needs being fixed.

The Epistle to the Hebrews admonishes us to not grow despondent or abandon the struggle (Heb 12:3). Realize some of your anger is justified, not just against our own failed religious leaders but also against the liberal press's perennial anti-Catholicism. Allow yourself to express your anger in appropriate ways: Speak the truth, write a letter, vote with your pocketbook.

How about setting out to renew yourself and purify the church? A good idea to consider is to begin to pray harder than you or I ever have in the past for God to take matters into his own hands. And remember, too, practicing constructive self-restraint involves meditating on the word of God. Consider the words of St. Paul on this topic:

> It is actually reported that there is sexual immorality among you, and of a kind that is not found even among pagans....[A]nd as if present I have already passed judgment in the name of the Lord Jesus....[Y]ou are to hand this man over to Satan. (1 Cor 5:1-5)

So do not be afraid to speak out.

> For you know what instructions we gave you through the Lord Jesus. For this is the will of God...that you abstain from fornication.... [W]hoever rejects this rejects not human authority, but God. (1 Thess 4:2–8)

Do not pay attention to anyone who says the contrary.

> [T]here will be false teachers among you, who will secretly bring in destructive opinions....[M]any will follow their licentious ways....And in their

greed they will exploit you with deceptive words. (2 Pet 2:1–3)

They may even be religion teachers or pastors.

For false messiahs and false prophets will appear and produce great signs and omens, to lead astray, if possible, even the elect. (Matt 24:24)

This is also true today.

But when Cephas came to Antioch, I opposed him to his face, because he stood self-condemned.... [B]ut when I saw that they were not acting consistently with the truth of the gospel, I said to Cephas before them all, "If you, though a Jew, live like a Gentile and not like a Jew, how can you compel the Gentiles to live like Jews?" (Gal 2:11–14)

Do not be afraid to assume your rightful role as a layperson in the Church.

Even if we or an angel from heaven should proclaim to you a gospel contrary to what we proclaimed to you, let that one be accursed. (Gal 1:8)

We have plenty of "false gospels" today.

Practicing constructive self-restraint involves reading about the great reform movements of times past: Caesar of Arles, St. Francis, St. Dominic, St. Catherine of Siena, St. Charles Borromeo, St. Francis de Sales, St. Ignatius, and so many others. They had to purify the church and they did so.

97

Practicing self-restraint involves familiarity with the councils that reformed the church. Most of the councils dealt with abuses in the church.

Learning from the Past

Start with the famous modern Church historian Henri Daniel-Rops. His *History of the Church* graphically describes situation after situation in the history of Europe where cultural and environmental circumstances gave birth to immoral behavior. Consider the situation of the church in the year 1000 as Daniel-Rops describes it:

> The men of that age had good reason to be disturbed. Material conditions were a source of anguish, and collective suffering is rarely a school of virtue. Imagine what life was like when every day might bring the Normans, the Saracens, or the leathern jackets of the Hungarian squadrons. This constant fear of impending catastrophe, so familiar to the twentieth century through the aerial bombardment of cities, that anxiety which blends with every sentiment, with all reactions of the conscience, and ends by obliterating everything else, was the psychological keynote of those generations, though as yet, perhaps, slower to act upon boorish, elemental souls in an age when no real protection was conceivable.[6]

If that is not bad enough, Daniel-Rops says:

> Violence, however, was not the only source of fear; there was not only danger of being slain by Barbarian raiders. The result of the new invasions

(as well as of feudal wars) was a terrible decline of agriculture since the days of Charlemagne. The work of breaking up the land for tillage was interrupted. In the most fertile plains, forest, heath, and marsh resumed the offensive. Moreover famine was rife on that badly cultivated land, the produce of which was continually threatened.[7]

Daniel-Rops notes that moral decadence was widespread:

Sexual immorality was found everywhere: among the lower classes, where the material conditions of life were such as to excuse the more bestial practices, and among the feudal lords also, whose luxury was allied with violence, as female prisoners too often experienced....The most serious feature of the whole set-up was that this demoralization did not spare the clergy, which was not infrequently caught up in the whirlwind of unbridled passion.[8]

Daniel-Rops gives us a good lesson in avoiding cynicism and purifying the church:

It is unnecessary to add that the crisis of sexual immorality which we have seen rampant among laymen ravaged the clergy likewise. It is a picture upon which many anti-Christian historians have been pleased to dwell, and unfortunately it is quite authentic. One need only read the conciliar decrees to be convinced of the extent of the evil (and of course the existence of such decrees indicates that there were still many healthy elements in the Church).

In 909 the Council of Trosly had quite rightly said that "wicked priests who rot on the dunghill of luxury infect by their conduct all those who live chastely, for the faithful are all too prone to think, 'Such are the priests of the Church.'"[9]

The councils of Anze (994) and Poitiers (1000) repeated those decisions, and in that of Pavia (1023) Pope Benedict VIII himself publicly denounced the morals of the clergy.

What lessons can we learn from history? Side by side with this immoral behavior is the history of the holiness of so many great saints and so many reformers who lived in those days. So you and I have a chance in our time to make a difference, just as St. Stephen of Hungary and others did in their day.

One of the great pages of Christian history was written at that time. There emerged in Hungary the glorious figure of St. Stephen, and all the sovereigns who afterwards reigned at Budapest considered it a point of honor to claim the spiritual heritage whose name, until recently, the crown of Hungary bore.[10]

Some Steps to Consider

Begin by deepening our relationship with the Lord. Keep repeating Paul's exhortation: "[B]e strong in the Lord and in the strength of his power....For our struggle is not against enemies of blood and flesh, but against the rulers, against the authorities, against the cosmic powers of this present darkness, against the spiritual forces of evil in the heavenly places" (Eph 6:10–12).

Remember to reduce the triggers in our lives and practice noncynical responses to trigger mechanisms. Constant practice builds success and the more instances of success we experience the better we feel about ourselves and the better we are able to help purify the church.

Cynicism in Families

Another example of cynicism corroding our spirituality is found in the vast number of dysfunctional families. Cynicism that has taken root in our families' dysfunctionality easily mutates into cynicism about our church in the face of so many media attacks and the failure of the clergy.

For a person to become successful in overcoming cynicism, there is a series of things that need to happen. First, the individual needs to learn to take charge of one's own life. Starting with a *trigger analysis* would be helpful here. What is it that you can do to reduce cynical attitudes? Let's look at some first steps.

The more a person can remove as many triggers as possible, the more likely it is at the beginning you will gain further strength to take charge of your life.

In the area of *setting events*, one needs to talk positively with someone who can help. If a family does not allow cynical putdowns of brothers and sisters toward each other, it has a better chance of being a caring family, one that stops cynicism before it even gets started. A family that has family meetings has a better chance of being caring, a family where spirituality can flourish. Just as horseplay in a family often leads to anger and angry outbursts, so, too, cynicism in a family leads to resentments and unhappiness.

There is a positive side to all of this. A family that eats tasty meals together and learns how to have good conversations has a better chance of caring for one another. A family that thanks mom for making the extra-special tasty meals is a family that has a better chance of keeping God in their hearts and cynicism at bay. In other words, warmth and effective praise by all members of the family can set a general atmosphere conducive to keeping cynicism in the alley and not in the house.

POSSIBLE POSITIVE ACTIONS

As previously mentioned, constructive self-restraint means not only using noncynical responses to *trigger events* but also moving toward *positive actions*. The following list suggests a few actions or reinforcers available to your family.

First, there are consumable reinforcers: a tasty brunch after church, a favorite dessert, a surprise dinner out. There are also activity reinforcers: going fishing, picnicking, going to the movies or the zoo, a ball game, a walk in the park. There are possessional reinforcers: a new dress, a new jacket, a new pair of shoes, a new game. And there are social reinforcers: spending time with someone special, visiting grandma, or reading bedtime stories.

Each of these is a step toward a better world free of the virus that makes people cynical. Success in constructive self-restraint within the family can lead to similar success in responding to the anti-Catholic attitudes of our friends. One success leads to another.

In summary, there are four action steps we can all practice to move beyond cynicism. They will help you bridge the gaps in your life and make everything reconnect with greater energy.

1. Remove as many negative setting events as possible. This will increase the likelihood of a happy outcome, reducing cynicism.
2. Practice noncynical responses to trigger mechanisms. If you cannot change the setting events, you can learn the appropriate response to trigger mechanisms. Practice makes perfect here. When you read another bitter story of clerical betrayal in the press, say to yourself: St. Francis and St. Clare purified the church of their time and so can we if we join together. The more instances we have of success in responding constructively to trigger mechanisms, the better we begin to feel about ourselves. And the better we begin to feel about ourselves, the more we are motivated to join others in what needs fixing. And the more we are motivated to respond constructively, the better role models we become. This tends to have a snowball effect.

   Start with reminding ourselves on a regular basis of the atmosphere we desire to create, namely, one conducive to cooperation and lacking in cynicism. Remember: The beginning always starts with praying regularly, perseveringly, and intensely for the strength and courage to begin.
3. Change your pattern of behavior to reduce the opportunity for *setting events* and *trigger mechanisms.* For example, stop reading every negative story about the church. Sometimes just changing where you sit or where you stand has a good effect. Or change when you come home or when you watch TV or

when you pray. When the main course is not to your liking, pick out one thing, perhaps a salad that you like. When two students irritate each other in your classroom, it is better to change seating so they are at opposite ends of the room. When someone makes a mess in the kitchen, distract yourself with busy work or go into the other room.

4. Finally, learn to provide an effective response to cynical comments or actions. The response should be immediate: "Wait a minute. I love the church and I will not let you get away with such bitter criticism." Or you might redirect the conversation, giving a more appropriate positive response: "Yes, it is awful. But if we work together, the Lord has promised us the help we need to make things better. We all know that we are the good Lord's hands and heart and mind right here where we live today." If inappropriate behavior continues, I have found from long experience that it is a good idea very politely to ask the perpetrators to please stop. When they respond positively to you, remember their response is worthy of recognition and praise. Thank them for seeing the positive side of things. Remind them that all your lives are better this way and encourage all to go in the right direction. Be sure to rehearse in advance what you might say, or even write it out on a little sheet of paper. Lots of folks have found this helpful.

In conclusion the degree to which you gain self-control when cynicism abounds is the degree to which you begin to feel better about renewal and reform in our beloved church. You begin to feel a little more in charge of your world; you begin to feel capable even of encouraging change in the concrete environment in which you live, where, with a little effort, you can make sure there are fewer triggers, fewer setting events, and more opportunities for positive interaction. Our spirituality becomes more mature and the church a better place when we learn self-control, just as there is positive growth wherever cynicism and misery are removed from our lives.

As you can see there is much asceticism involved in these behavioral practices and they can help to build a world of hope.

Chapter 6

IDEALISM VERSUS IDEOLOGY

Ours is an age of people embracing movements, causes, slogans, and mantras, using them to explain everything and making them the center of their lives. Both young people and adults face the fourth secular challenge of ideology, one of the predominant characteristics of our times. The remedy is to rediscover Christian idealism.

SOME INITIAL CONSIDERATIONS

As a boy I remember being surprised to learn that there was something called "fool's gold." To the untrained eye it looked like gold, but it was not the real thing. Ideology is the fool's gold of our times and mass media makes it enormously attractive. It is aided by other cultural forces such as mediocrity in education and superficiality of lifestyles. It is especially seductive to the very poor and the very rich.

This chapter will look at a number of ideologies typical of the postmodern culture as we try to explain how they work and why they are fool's gold.

What is ideology? It is a negative process excluding or blocking consideration of large amounts of data and reducing one's vision to a single, narrow focus. It is an exclusive focus on only one idea by which everything is explained, like a set of glasses allowing you to see only one object. It is an aberration.

Now we all need to focus in order to see things in life. If our eyes do not focus, our vision is blurred; so focusing is a positive event. We can get a wide-angle view of the world from space and that is helpful at times. The use of a microscope reduces or narrows the field of vision so that the focus or concentration is totally on a very small area. That is also sometimes helpful.

Ideology, however, is like using a microscope for everything; you have access to other information but you are not using it. You are not seeing anything except the magnified object in your microscope. Only using a microscope is a bad choice. If you do it enough times it becomes a habit that hurts instead of helps.

Ideology is like a small, dark lens through which we see the world. If you let it dominate your thinking, your view of the world becomes an aberration and your thoughts are jaundiced.

IDEOLOGY AND IDEOLOGUES

Ideology was developed into a fine art in the last century when Nazism, Marxism, and Leninism were prime examples of a new way of thinking in which people were taught to hate.

An ideologue primarily has no interest whatsoever in dialogue or cooperating with those holding a different viewpoint. One tends to despise others and is usually unwilling to see or consider their point of view. Even if one has access to other information, one does not bother using it. You cannot see anything else but this evil, including the misuse of authority, and destroying that authority becomes a right, even an imperative. If one engages in this kind of ideological thinking over and over again, it becomes an obsession, dominating one's life: your thinking, your feelings, your whole existence. You think hateful thoughts, have hateful feelings, and do hateful things. You oppose every authority figure except, of course, yourself and your fellow ideologues.

Starting in the 1960s ideology assumed a more central role in the Christian churches of America, with conservatives and progressives increasingly at war with each other.

On September 11, 2001, most Americans were shaken to the core of their being by the terrorist attacks on the World Trade Center and the Pentagon. A new ideology made its presence known to America and to the world.

For the first time, Americans looked seriously at Osama bin Laden's *fatwa* issued February 1998. It is a classic example of ideology in our time:

> *The ruling to kill the Americans and their allies—civilians and military—is an individual duty for every Muslim who can do it in any country in which it is possible to do it, in order to liberate the al-Aqsa Mosque [of Jerusalem] and the Holy Mosque [of Mecca] from their grip, and in order for their armies to move out of all the lands of Islam....We—with God's help—call on every Muslim who believes in God and wishes to be rewarded to comply with God's order to kill the Americans and plunder their money wherever and whenever they find it.*[1]

In the last half of the twentieth century we have experienced in America a series of movements that gave birth to some very strident ideologues. The movements themselves were not ideologies, but ideologues sprang from their bosom. Let us take several examples.

The antiwar movement which was so influential in the late 1960s and early 1970s produced good, honest leaders but also its share of ideologues with an exclusive narrow focus, namely, one idea, a government waging an unjust war, and through this lens everything else was explained. One of the chief by-products of ideologues of that period was hatred of our country and self-loathing. Although the antiwar movement did not need ideologues to succeed, it had them anyway. The movement fortunately did bring down an ill-fated administration and did successfully put an end to one of the saddest pages in American history, namely, an unwise and unsuccessful venture in Southeast Asia where we were heirs to the French and British colonial rule. In the process, powerful ideologues seem to have adversely affected the lives of the young generation.

Similarly, the civil rights movement of the late 1960s and early 1970s made massive gains for so many people and most especially helped the nation become better than before. The movement had a large share of passionate, dedicated, and marvelous people, but also its share of ideologues.

What is amazing is that a man like Martin Luther King would come along who was clearly not an ideologue but rather a Christian idealist. Whatever otherwise might have been his faults, he walked a thin and noble line on the issue of discrimination and invited many others to follow him on the road of nonviolence. His was the way of invitation to cooperation, for he did not go around looking at every turn for authority to defy, even though he defied authority. He did not go around looking at every turn for people to be angry at, even though he was angry at people. He did not go around resisting all authority figures. And he surely did not preach hatred; he preached love of God and love of neighbor.

POLARIZATION AND ITS EFFECTS

In these difficult historical times, polarization within the U.S. Catholic Church between two distinct and identifiable groups, progressive and conservative, seems to have been at work. In hindsight the way in which Vatican II was implemented seems to have played a lasting religious role in this country.

Cardinal Ratzinger (now Benedict XVI) said in 1984: "It is my opinion that the misfortunes the Church has met with in the last 20 years are not due to the True Council itself, but to an unleashing within the Council of latent aggressive political and centrifugal forces."[2]

When does this become ideology? When it crosses over to the dark mystique of holding the true council is the problem. One of these groups calls themselves traditionalists and this is their self-description:

- "A traditionalist is nothing more or less then a Catholic who continues to worship as Catholics have always and to believe as Catholics have always believed until approximately 1965, when in the name of Vatican II, the Church began to undergo a series of unprecedented reforms that altered every aspect of ecclesiastical life."[3]
- "Traditionalists continue to regard the Church as Catholics had always been taught to regard her before

1965: That is the one true Church to which separated brethren must return...."[4]

- "The Traditionalist maintains that in point of fact, no Catholic is obliged to embrace a single one of the novelties imposed upon the Church over the past 35 years."[5]
- "A Traditionalist is someone who believes that the post conciliar novelties, especially the new liturgy and the new ecumenism ought to be abandoned because they have caused great harm to the Church, as shown by overwhelming empirical evidence of drastic decline in nearly every area immediately following the appearance of the novelties."[6]

The litmus test is Vatican II. If any bishop or priest praises Vatican II, the traditionalists are filled with anger. They consider as traitors anyone who thinks contrary to their view. This issue of Vatican II dominates their lives and that is the definition of ideology.

A second example of ideologues today can be found within our two major political parties, the Democrats and the Republicans. Few would deny that among the Republicans, Donald Rumsfeld is one of those ideologues. Many Catholics are Republicans because of the party's promotion of the culture of life. At the same time, these Catholics are saddened by the image of Enron and WorldCom executives and so many other CEOs flaunting huge riches, while the party condemns welfare mothers. So many Catholics feel almost compelled to vote for pro-life Republicans, even though the party seems to care little about reigning in corporate greed. Neither does the party seem to make a big deal about huge corporations making enormous sums in the cause of Operation Iraqi Freedom. Recall Franklin Roosevelt in World

War II chastising corporations for what he called "war profiteering."

The days when Catholic and Democrat were synonymous seem long gone. Why? For the simple reason that ideologues seem to have gained control of much of the Democratic Party and their shrill voices prevail regarding abortion on demand and other culture-of-death issues. It is almost as if these Democrats have given greater voice and greater credence to the fringe elements of our society, celebrating those on the cutting edge of social change, more than assisting those who are marginalized. Governor Robert Casey, a Democrat of Pennsylvania, was denied an opportunity to speak at the Democratic National Convention for the very simple reason that he was a strong pro-life Democrat. Since Roe v. Wade, more children in America have been killed in the womb than the entire population of Canada. There are ideologues who use their power to silence Bob Casey and others who disagree with them.

Father Frank DeSiano, former president of the Paulist Fathers, recently noted: "We Catholics are all dressed up, 62 million of us, but feeling we have no party to go to."[7] That is not an excuse for us to neglect politics and our participation in public life. It is rather an invitation to grow stronger and wiser in and through our participation.

A third example of ideologues can be found within the environmental movement. There are plenty of good people in the environmental movement who are not ideologues and who care about both human life and God's good creation. Consider Hurricane Katrina as an example of ideology partially at work. Hurricane Katrina was said to be a category 5 storm when it hit New Orleans and the worst hurricane in history.

An article in *Popular Mechanics* stated: "Though many accounts portray Katrina as a storm of unprecedented magnitude, it was in fact a large, but otherwise typical hurricane."[8] It reached landfall in New Orleans as a midlevel category 3 storm. As the article noted: "Winds in the city barely reached hurricane strength." Many early media reports were later found to be in error.

Why then was Hurricane Katrina such an enormous disaster? In a 2006 book entitled *Eco-Freaks*, John Berlau, of the Competitive Enterprise Group, says, "Because of environmental restrictions, state and local officials in charge of flood control were thwarted from building the structures that would have best protected New Orleans from storm surges and hurricanes."[9] Berlau notes that back in 1965: "Right after Hurricane Betsy, there was a consensus that something beyond levees must be constructed to withstand nature's wrath on the Crescent City. With the backing of Louisiana's congressional delegation and the levee board of New Orleans, both of which were almost exclusively of Democratic persuasion, the US Army Corps of Engineers proposed large steel and concrete gates—to be built primarily in the water—to block storm surge....The structures would have operated like the 'sea gates' then being built in the Netherlands, which are also below sea level, to protect cities from North Sea storms."[10]

Joe Towers with the New Orleans District of The Army Corps of Engineers (1965–96) said, "The purpose of the proposed gates was to prevent hurricane force winds from driving storm surges into the lake (Pontchartrain) and then blowing them south and into the City of New Orleans....If we had built the barriers, New Orleans would not be flooded."[11]

What happened then is interesting. In 1977, when the Corps of Engineers was about to build these gates, a new law was passed, The National Environmental Policy Act (NEPA), which stated an individual citizen could petition to stop a government project considered bad for the environment if a judge agreed with that citizen. That is what happened. Save Our Wetlands used NEPA to stop the project.[12] Environmentalists can appear at times to place a great value on the life of animals, birds, forests, and global warming and do not share a similar concern for the sanctity of human life. Saving seals is noble but how about a similar concern for unborn human children?

The purpose of saying all of this is to illustrate the fact that in many of these issues, the waters are muddied by ideologists.

LIVING BY IDEOLOGIES

"Woe to you, scribes and Pharisees, hypocrites! For you cross sea and land to make a single convert, and you make the new convert twice as much a child of hell as yourselves." (Matt 23:15)

We have all seen an obsessed football fan and how painful he makes others' lives. Much more painful are those who live by ideology. Ideologues of the left or the right are not as radical as they may appear to be. They are just people who have lost their way. In many cases their hearts start off in the right place, filled with care, filled with concern, filled with goodness. Anger has a strange way of consuming people, whether of the left or of the right. Negative behavior in isolation alienates people and they become truly lonely and unhappy.

What do ideologues look like? They have a sense of belonging with other like-minded citizens and the common bond is constant unhappiness. They maintain this constant unhappiness for the simple reason that ideologies are so narrow, so confining and so extreme. Since ideologies are insatiable, such an afflicted person rarely says things are okay.

They are unable to perceive correctly the behavior and intentions of those around them. They are suspicious, almost paranoid, and constantly untrusting. They say loyalty is what they need, but what they want is fanaticism. They want you to read only the right books and the right newspapers and join the right groups, to stay pumped up with suspicions, paranoia, and lack of trust.

An ideology must have wrongs, real or imagined, accurate or exaggerated, to generate the emotions necessary for the obsession and extreme actions every ideology demands. An ideology itself becomes a totalitarian symbol much greater than those it opposes so indiscriminately.

An ideology fixates on the past, calling up known wrongs and filling the void between wrongs with conspiracies and "new facts" to make every past wrong bigger than life, bigger than it really was. The ideologist calls for actions today to redress wrongs of the past and these actions are often destructive and vengeful rather than restorative or progressive. Martin Luther King did no such thing. He called for changes now and for the future. He called for people to go to the places that were relevant to his day and make improvements there.

An idealist is one who calls us to care for one another as the Lord cares for us. A Christian idealist says that building a society based on hatred is to build a house that will destroy itself in the end.

When ideologies are given total power and authority, history gives them names—totalitarianism, Nazism, Fascism, Communism. However, where there is no consistent leadership, and no guiding goals or principles, history calls them anarchy, riot, mayhem, and terrorism.

Ideological behaviors are not the basic message of Jesus Christ, for he did not say, "Become weird for my sake." He said, "Follow me" (Matt 4:19).

This involves steering a middle course between the ideologies of the left and of the right. If we really love God and love our neighbor we will be moved to personal renewal and institutional purification of the church. These will not come about by embracing ideologies whether of the left or the right. Yet that is the agenda we hear so often proposed. We can readily educate ourselves in this matter. Personal renewal and institutional purification will come about through those who love the Lord enough and their brothers and sisters enough to do something without ideology and in accord with scripture and tradition even if it requires great sacrifice in following the Lord.

SOME QUESTIONS TO CONSIDER

In summary, if we want to know whether we are on the road to becoming an ideologue, let us ask a few basic questions. Are we alienated from the vast majority of those who follow the gospel? Are we living as sectarians? Have people said that one of our principal characteristics is anger and cynicism and even hatred? Have people said that we seem to take joy in defying authority? Is our conversation filled exclusively with cynical, cutting remarks especially about the church and those in authority? Do we feel the world is filled with more wrongs than rights and that few care? Do we feel that as the new millennium opened we crossed the threshold of despair, not the threshold of hope?

Do we see things through a dark lens? Do we have no wide-angle view of the world? Does this sound like the basic message of Jesus Christ, which is to love God and love your neighbor? Let us try to polish up our ideals of love of God and love of neighbor by following the Christian life prescribed in the gospels. Such a Christian idealist is like a spark igniting action, a beacon of hope in tough times.

Chapter 7
LEARNED HELPLESSNESS

"There is nothing I can do to make things better."

If cynicism and ideology are powerful characteristics of the postmodern era, learned helplessness is another secular challenge to be faced. Its remedy is a can-do attitude, called self-efficacy. Learned helplessness keeps one from trying, from doing battle with evil, from setting out on the journey to the mountain to throw the ring into the fire, from standing up for what is right. No one can grow spiritually or renew the church if they have learned to be helpless. Deepening of spirituality cannot take root in our lives if one believes, *"This is the way things are and there is nothing I can do about it."* Learned helplessness takes many shapes and forms.

SOME EXAMPLES

Here at Boys Town we see this helplessness all the time in the lives of our young children. Children at age twelve or fourteen or sixteen are saying they cannot change because *"that's the way things are."*

Bill, fourteen, says, "My father abandoned us when I was four and my mother chose drugs and alcohol over me and when she abandoned me I started skipping school and drinking. There is nothing I can do about my life."

Little twelve-year-old LaKisha says, "I have never been able to read very well because I am not good in school and there is nothing I can do about it."

Joseph, sixteen, says, "I was sexually abused as a child and that is why I sexually abuse others. That is my way of life and there is nothing I can do about it."

Guadalupe comments, "My mother slept around and my two sisters do the same. That is my life too and there is nothing I can do about it."

Juan says with resignation, "I have a violent temper just as my dad did. My mother was pushy and selfish and that is why I'm pushy and selfish. And there is nothing I can do about it."

In these troubling times in the church, one sees various types of people from all backgrounds resigning themselves to the fact that there is nothing they can do about the situation, so why try. Think of so many people mired in poverty or sickness, totally without hope, or so many chemically dependent people who believe they have no future, so many white-collar workers in countless corporations who "go along to get along." Teachers also know the phenomenon very well. They see learned helplessness in their classrooms. They have seen so many students who have given up hope and are afraid to try. Doctors see patients who have given up hope, do not want to get well, and do not get well.

The story of a teachers' union whose leaders came to the bargaining table saying that the low morale of their members was due to the labor contract stipulating student evaluation of each teacher as part of their overall annual performance review comes to mind. One of the teachers summed it all up by saying that he knew it was just a matter of time before the students would get him. "I have tried and tried and tried, but I know in the end the students will make me look bad, so there is no sense trying."

For whatever reason, this teacher believes there is nothing he can do. Sooner or later he will receive a failing evaluation. This attitude of learned helplessness can even permeate a whole classroom where there is no excitement or no willingness to try to learn math or science. There is just the humdrum of waiting for the inevitable.

Many Christians in our time have been brought low by an outbreak of learned helplessness at a time when scandal after scandal has swept through the Catholic Church filling newspapers with lurid details and talk shows with grim stories. This perception of learned helplessness has spread at a time when many good parents are looking in disbelief as their children are subjected to what they consider misguided educational ideologies of the left or right. Here are some symptoms of this attitude: being overwhelmed with feelings of helplessness, an unwillingness to try to change things, a sense that it won't do any good. There is nothing I can do to make things better, so I will retreat into the inner sanctuary of my own work.

PAST LESSONS

During the Great Depression of the 1930s, as many as one out of three American workers were unemployed due to a set of economic factors beyond their control. Part of Franklin Roosevelt's New Deal consisted of creating jobs. Among those jobs a number of out-of-work professors were employed surveying people's attitudes toward their plight. These studies were filed away in government archives and gathered dust for decades.

In the 1970s Dr. Martin P. Seligman and other behavioral psychologists at Penn State who were looking into the phenomenon of learned helplessness discovered this treasure trove of data.[1] It gave them the opportunity to go back and interview some of these same people years later. Seligman and his fellow researchers wanted to find out who overcame their plight and who did not, and whether there were any significant differences in these groups. They looked especially hard at people who lost everything in the Depression and, even when good times returned, never recovered. It seemed these people learned to be helpless. "Learned helplessness is the giving-up reaction, the quitting response that follows from the belief that whatever you do doesn't matter."[2]

There were three common characteristics of the group of people who never recovered.

1. **Permanence—***The bad events will last a long time/ forever.*
   Those who never bounced back saw their troubles as permanent. The loss of work and wealth and the absence of business opportunity were not seen as a temporary setback because times were bad. Quite the opposite. This group believed that they would never regain what they had before and, even when prosperity returned, they felt doomed. The loss of job and livelihood was such a shock that they were sure they would just never make it. This turned out to be a self-fulfilling prophecy. Long decades later they were interviewed and their lives had not amounted to much.

2. **Pervasiveness**—*This will undermine everything I do.*
These same people who did not bounce back from the Depression even when good times came also saw their troubles as not only affecting one area but all areas of their lives. It was not solely that they had lost their farm and would not get another one. It was rather that they had lost everything and would never amount to anything in life. This form of overdramatizing is called catastrophizing. They did not look upon the Depression as a temporary disappointment. They saw it as a pervasive catastrophe embracing their whole life.

3. **Personal**—*These bad events are my own fault.*
In the midst of the troubles, while they see others succeeding, they tend to blame themselves for their failure to bounce back. There may be other factors, but none they see as decisive as their own inadequacies. They do not look for an adequate explanation in other sources such as deflation or poor economic planning. They would complain about the poor economy and the high unemployment, but saw others prospering with jobs. So they told themselves that deep down it was their own fault they could not find a job. Perhaps they had not studied enough or learned enough or been adventurous enough or something. It was their own fault they did not have an education. They could not make a good living. It was their own fault they were not successful with their family. We made this mess ourselves. It was not imposed on us from the outside. These pessimistic people lived a life of helplessness.

These three characteristics seem applicable to many in our church today. Are you convinced that the church's troubles are not short-lived but will last a long time (permanent) and will undermine everything you do (pervasive)? And you could have done something about it but did not (personal)? Professor Seligman calls this a pessimistic explanatory style. It spreads helplessness.

A VICIOUS CIRCLE

Hopeless thoughts are followed by hopeless feelings resulting in hopeless behavior. It is a vicious circle. Confronted by the troubles of our church, such people give up easily and get depressed more often.

We see this all the time with our boys and girls here at Boys Town. They express their hopelessness in many ways. Janet was born in prison, her mother being a convicted drug dealer. Abandoned, Janet lived in thirteen places before she came to us at age sixteen with the attitude: I have tried but nothing works and nobody cares.

Kids say they want to control their anger, but "I just can't do it." They say they have tried to learn math, but "it just doesn't do any good." "Nothing I tried in the past ever helped me learn how to do well in school, so I have stopped trying."

Learned helplessness is difficult to overcome because it is the bitter fruit of experience. More often than not when kids come to us, they see school as a place of failure. No wonder they hate school, for who would want to go every day to a place where you know you are going to fail?

The addiction process is another instance where helplessness is learned with predictable results. One of our boys told the following story. He had just arrived at Boys Town and had accepted an invitation to a Living without Chemicals meeting. Our chaplain had scheduled a speaker who did not show because of car trouble. The chaplain had to fill in and, even though he doesn't do this often, he told the kids the story of his own plunge into alcohol addiction many years ago. He told about a life of lying and drinking and not being able to stop no matter what he did and no matter what he tried. He said he was simply hopeless and that nothing worked until someone took him to an AA meeting. Slowly, he began to walk the road to recovery.

A boy wrote a note to the priest afterwards and said, "My whole family is alcoholic. I am fourteen and have been drinking for three years. I tried to stop, but couldn't. I had given up all hope. But then you told your story and for the first time in many years I said to myself: Maybe there is hope for me."

Then I think about all the teachers, youth ministers, and catechists who somehow or other repeatedly heard from their parents, teachers, and peers that they are not smart and they will never learn anything. Well, they did learn something; they learned helplessness and they feel helpless to move the church toward renewal in the midst of its current troubles. This learned helplessness saps spiritual vitality and inhibits spiritual growth.

They do not read the scriptures with any sense of confidence due to being convinced that only scripture scholars can really profit from the scriptures.

So many say to themselves, "My relationship with the Lord will never amount to anything." How their spiritual lives suffer. And when terrible troubles and scandals come to the church as they have in our times, so many tell themselves there is nothing they can do about this.

FIVE SYMPTOMS OF LEARNED HELPLESSNESS IN OUR SPIRITUAL LIVES TODAY

1. *A superficial lifestyle.* If I have little or no hope, why would I think of renewing my spiritual life or purifying the church? Why not concentrate on things like golf, the soaps, the NFL, the NASCAR circuit, or shopping? Why would I bother to read anything substantial or try to learn anything of value? Why should I try to be courageous? After all, what good would that do?

2. *Loss of initiative.* Hopelessness dashes cold water on the fires of initiative. It makes it harder and harder even to try, so the leader inside of you stays there and never comes out. "Why bother? It won't do any good anyway." Learned helplessness is quite different from laziness. There are lots of bright people in the world who are intellectually lazy and who never had to exert a lot of effort in school because things came easily for them. This is their whole reinforcement history, namely, they never had to work hard to get acceptable results and this keeps intellectual laziness alive. Learned helplessness is not laziness; it is a loss of heart. It is forgetting the Lord's words: "[T]ake courage; I have conquered the world!" (John 16:33).

3. *Nothing works and nobody cares.* A helpless person can easily become a source of discouragement to others. In other words, the contagion can spread and the negative attitude is passed on to others. Such negativism can infect a parish, a monastery, a convent, and a whole diocese, resulting in unhappiness and

dissention. Once helplessness infects a follower of the Lord or a group of followers it corrodes hope. It blots out memories, neutralizes grace, and stifles happiness. Without memories of the Lord's "amazing grace" and hopes of "being there 10,000 years bright shining as the sun" there can be no reason to stay active in the community of believers, the church.

4. *Depression*. When we harbor convictions of helplessness, dark clouds appear. When we cling to pessimistic beliefs, we get discouraged. Too much fear and negative thinking makes us depressed.

5. *Don't join us*. If you are convinced that the situation is very bad and there is nothing you can do to make a difference, then you will surely not encourage vocations. The young will be turned off by your negative attitude for the simple reason that no one will want to join a group of hopeless people. The young are idealistic by nature; they want to make the world a better place. But you have already given up on trying to make the world a better place. It is no use. It will not work.

SELF-INVENTORY

The following is a self-inventory that each of us can take. It covers three major areas of life with the purpose of seeing if we are suffering from learned helplessness.

The first area is exploration of the reasons for your own inertia and sense of futility.

Take a look at your own lack of initiative in the face of the terrible troubles in the church where you live. Do you see these as a temporary setback in your life from which you will recover in the future, or as an unchangeable state of affairs?

- Do you take the initiative in troubles facing your family, your work, your ministry? Or do you just "do what I have to do"?
- Do you problem solve or let problems simmer and solve themselves?
- Do you see the terrible troubles in the church as something you can impact or not?
- Do you find your lack of initiative a temporary setback?
- Do you tell yourself: This is the way life is. There is nothing I can do about it.
- Do you feel you weren't a good student and never enjoyed learning?
- Or do you feel you are not trying hard enough and need to give it your best?

Much research has been done with young children and the feedback they receive from parents and teachers. For example, well-respected researcher Carol Dweck and her colleagues looked at what they called a typical third-grade classroom in which girls were routinely more polite, more attentive, and more cooperative and boys were routinely more off task, more easily distracted, and less cooperative.[3] They studied remediation: why boys doing poorly recovered more readily than girls doing poorly.

As a result of this typical behavior pattern, a common explanation by teachers for the boys' test failure centered around their lack of attention:

> *"You did not pay attention and therefore failed."* (a temporary state of affairs)
> *"You are not trying hard enough."* (a changeable state of affairs)
> *"You did not give it your best."* (again this is changeable)

The situation a boy finds himself in can then be remedied by starting to pay attention and trying harder. The message to the boys is that, when they fail, the next time they need to pay more attention and try harder because failure is something that can be remedied and there is no reason to be hopeless. This advice contributes to a hopeful attitude.

On the other hand, the researchers found it more likely that a teacher would say to the girls:

> *"You always hand in sloppy papers."* (a permanent state of affairs)
> *"You are not very good at equations."* (an unchangeable state of affairs)

By the fourth grade, most girls who had heard these explanations gave up. They learned helplessness.

What about your own spiritual and moral life? Whatever afflicts you—lack of zeal, carelessness at Mass, neglect of personal prayers, becoming more selfish—do you see this as a temporary setback or the early onset of a permanent problem?

Are there times when you say to yourself you want to work for justice in the world and not just read about it? Are there times when you say you want to volunteer again at the homeless shelter as you used to and not just talk about it? Or would you like to, but you gave up when scandals hit the

Church? There are times when you say to yourself you want to pray the Divine Office every day and not skip so many days as you do. You would like to pray it every day because you promised the Lord you would do so when you made your vows. But you have skipped it now for quite a number of days and then for quite a number of weeks.

What do you say to yourself? This always happens when I get discouraged. I always forget. I am a procrastinator. I am never good at setting time aside. I never was a leader. That is the way God made me and I cannot change.

Or do you say to yourself: Yes, I am discouraged, but it is a temporary setback. I know I can set time aside. Yes, I did not try hard enough, but I will give it my best tomorrow.

Consider this self-fulfilling phrase: *"This is the way God made me and I cannot change."* How many times have I heard that from people in prison. Their dysfunctionality has become an accepted way of life rather than a personal challenge to be faced.

When you fail, do you say to yourself, "This is the way it is and I can't change," or do you say to yourself, "Yes, I have failed, but with the grace of God I can change and succeed"?

The first step: Write on an index card the words of St. Paul to Timothy to be "a good soldier of Christ Jesus" (2 Tim 2:3). Put it on your dresser and read it every morning and every night. In other words, with the help of God, I can change. I can press on to victory in the Lord. I will take the first step today.

A second question centers on your attitude toward the crisis in the church today. Is the crisis only affecting one area of your life or is it pervasive?

When we were little children our mothers were the most influential persons in our lives. We asked our mother all kinds of questions and many of her explanations were adopted by us and have stayed with us these long years. If you had a mother with a lot of hope, chances are that you became a pretty hopeful person as well.

Consider this example. I remember as a little boy walking to the corner grocery store with my mother to get a loaf of bread for the evening meal. I was very small and yet recall vividly that it was just after a summer rain burst and the storm clouds were moving toward the west covering the sun. My mother stopped and told me to look at the sun shining on the edges of the big dark cloud. She called it a "silver lining," and added, "Val, always remember to look for the silver lining when a cloud appears in the blue. You will know that somewhere the sun is shining. And it will shine for you."

I still remember that day and that moment and recall how happy my mother was. On that day she gave me a way to interpret the troubles that come into the lives of all of us and I have never forgotten it. Later I found out that these were the lyrics to a famous song of those days and even now when troubles come I look for the silver lining. Perhaps that is why I am deeply moved by the passage in Revelation that says, "God will wipe away every tear from their eyes" (7:17). So what is your attitude toward the crisis in the church today? What do you say to yourself?

Do you say that everything and everyone in the church is a mess? Or do you say to yourself that some church leaders have failed but not all? Are you willing to overcome the pervasive attitude of negativity and faultfinding and consider seeing the "bigger picture"? While there may be problems and difficulties, the church's marvelous sacramental life helps us overcome human weakness and failings on the personal, local, national, and universal levels.

Write St. Paul's words on a little index card: "I consider that the sufferings of this present time are not worth comparing with the glory about to be revealed to us" (Rom 8:18). Put that on your desk.

The third item of self-inventory looks at the meaning of my life.

It asks four questions:

- Who am I?
- Who are you?
- What am I doing here?
- What are you doing here?

In other words, *what is it all about?*

Working all these years with children, I have seen hundreds of sick and discouraged mothers who communicated that sense of discouragement to their children.

- Mom: *Who am I?* A sick person who is your mother.
- Child: *Who are you?* A child of a sick mom.
- Mom: *What am I doing here?* Spending my days being sick.
- Child: *What are you doing here?* Languishing in an environment of illness and disappointment.

Here at Boys Town we deal with countless children whom life has failed not at the end, not at the middle, but at the very beginning. They have been abandoned and abused and neglected. They have been lied to over and over again.

One of our boys told a story the other day about visiting his grandparents. His mom is in drug treatment and his dad is in the penitentiary for drug dealing. He and his grandparents were sitting at the table after supper and the topic of marijuana came up. The boy talked about times in the past when he had been caught smoking pot. So his grandfather got up and went into the bedroom, bringing out a dime bag, lighting it up for himself, and inviting his grandson to do the same.

I asked him how he felt when that happened and he said, "Kind of sick inside."

I have seen too many hurt and discouraged clergy, religious, and laity who have communicated that sense of learned helplessness by saying:

- *Who is the church?* A sick institution that cannot mother you.
- *And who are you?* I am a child of my sick church.
- *What is your church doing here?* Spending its days being sick.
- *What are you doing here?* Languishing in the environment of disappointment and hopelessness.

How do you feel when you hear this? Kind of sick inside. What is the remedy for this malady? You will find it in the lives of all the apostles, evangelists, and the great saints down thru the ages.

- *Who is the church?* God's people on pilgrimage sent by the Spirit to bring good news, yet suffering, dying, and rising, the body of Christ, God's sons and daughters, the followers of Jesus.
- *Who are you?* I am one of God's people together with others called and sent to bring good news, yet suffering.
- *What is your church doing here?* Bringing us food for the journey, preaching the good news to the poor, while recovering from a life-threatening illness.

- *What are you doing here?* Nourished by the heavenly food I, together with others, am helping many on the journey, especially the poor, and I am joining in the purification of our beloved church.

This is a description of self-efficacy, which Albert Bandura defines as "belief in one's capabilities to organize and execute the courses of action required to produce given attainments."[4] This is another and more academic way to describe a can-do attitude: You and I can help each other find our own motivation from the scriptures, our own thought processes through action, our own effectiveness through experience that we really can produce purification of ourselves and for the church.

We all know effective people who are not slow to take advantage of opportunities, quickly figuring out ways to get the job done by prayer and collective action. This is an exercise of social cognitive theory, which has the merit of moving beyond a dualism of self and environment into a richer view of a reciprocal triad: the external environment on one side, our behavior on the other side, and the thoughts and feelings interacting with them.

Those who would control us, those who are enemies of freedom, would have us believe that we cannot really make a difference. Yet Jesus' teaching in the gospels and the lives of the saints remind us that there is something we can do to make things better. How about giving this a try as a way to rejuvenate your spiritual life?

The old *Dutch Catechism* starts off with a story of where to look for the meaning of life.

In A.D. 627 the monk Paulinus visited King Edwin in northern England to persuade him to accept

Christianity. He hesitated and decided to summon his advisers. At the meeting one of them stood up and said: Your majesty, when you sit at table with your lords and vassals, in the winter when the fire burns warm and bright on the hearth and the storm is howling outside, bringing the snow and the rain, it happens of a sudden that a little bird flies into the hall. It comes in at one door and flies out through the other. For the few moments that it is inside the hall, it does not feel the cold, but as soon as it leaves your sight, it returns to the dark of winter. It seems to me that the life of man is much the same. We do not know what went before and we do not know what follows. If the new doctrine can speak to us surely of these things, it is well for us to follow it.[5]

SOME INITIAL STEPS FOR TERRIBLY TROUBLED TIMES

In troubled times of betrayal and ridicule, it is important to remember these cures for learned helplessness:

- I am not on the *Titanic*. This may be a horrible disappointment, a terrible time, but the ship won't sink.
- "[T]he gates of Hades will not prevail against it" (Matt 16:18).
- We can renew the church and we will.
- "[L]ift your drooping hands and strengthen your weak knees" (Heb 12:12).
- I can't do everything, but I can do something—the optimistic option—I can improve my prayer life. I

can improve relationships. Together we can make a difference.

- When troubles surround us, Hebrews exhorts us to "be strongly encouraged to seize the hope set before us. We have this hope, a sure and steadfast anchor of the soul" (Heb 6:18–19).

- Remember, there were two kinds of anchors in the ancient Mediterranean world. There was an anchor you threw overboard when you got to harbor. That's not the kind of anchor mentioned here. This anchor is the one that you toss overboard in the midst of a terrible storm while you are out to sea. It stabilizes the ship so that it will not sink. It is the anchor of hope.

- The Lord has sent me into the world on a mission and I know he always provides plenty of grace and help to carry out the mission.

- "I thank you, Father, Lord of heaven and earth, because you have hidden these things from the wise and intelligent and have revealed them to infants" (Matt 11:25).

Come Holy Spirit,
fill the hearts of Thy faithful
and kindle in them the fire of Thy love.
Send forth Thy Spirit and they shall be created
and Thou shalt renew the face of the earth.

Chapter 8

ANTI-INTELLECTUALISM

"Let us do the thinking for you."

In the cold war era, Aleksandr Solzhenitsyn smuggled out of the Soviet Union a huge work entitled *The Gulag Archipelago*, which met with enormous success. One of its chief themes was all-encompassing mind control. A Lithuanian friend of mine sums up his Soviet life in those days with two rules. Rule #1: Trust no one. Rule #2: Fear everyone. In other words, let the Party do the thinking for you.

In many ways, this observation seems to become evident in the underlying message of the mass media: *Let us do the thinking for you.* This is the sixth secular challenge to be met, anti-intellectualism. The primary remedy is to be attentive to this prevailing societal attitude and to rediscover learning.

SOME PRELIMINARY CONSIDERATIONS

Advertising tries to effect what many of us desire to buy. News commentators can greatly influence our thoughts and what to think. Movies and videos impact upon our feelings and how we act. The secular message can almost become an alternative invitation to the gospel message: "Come, follow me." This anti-intellectual culture has deeply influenced our religious lives.

In an article entitled, "True and False Reform," Cardinal Avery Dulles reminds us that the First Vatican Council "successfully eliminated…certain reform movements of the 19th Century."[1] He continues by noting, "As a result, the Papacy maintained uncontested control of the Catholic Church through the middle of the 20th Century."[2]

The positive side of this centralized control was an outpouring of spiritual vitality resulting from the elimination of Gallicanism and the conciliar movement. However, the negative side was a slow, numbing anti-intellectualism summed up by the phrase: *"Let us do the thinking for you."* It may appear that even the institutional church conveyed this sense.

The benefit of solidarity with Catholics across the world was often at the cost of numbing conformity; the unencumbered faith was sometimes at the cost of closed mindedness. Uniformity was almost at the cost of individuality and honesty of expression. Yes, let us do the thinking for you.

In the late 1960s came the civil rights movement and the anti-Vietnam War protests with their emphasis on individual freedom, openness of approach, and honesty of expression. These strong winds were also blowing through the church, whose windows had been flung open by Blessed Pope John XXIII. What blew in the window was not always real learning, but in addition various ersatz cultural values of the times.

Vatican II's *Church in the Modern World* specifically praised psychology and sociology. Among the major points cited:

> Advances in…psychology and the social sciences
> not only lead man to greater self-awareness, but

provide him with the technical means of molding the lives of whole peoples as well.[3]

Recent psychological advances furnish further insights into human behavior.[4]

In pastoral care, sufficient use should be made, not only of the theological principles, but also of the findings of secular sciences, especially psychology and sociology.[5]

This historical time was one for intellectual posturing by and for the social sciences. Harvey Cox wrote *The Secular City*, telling us that God had no place in urban life. Many came to believe that our society would soon be secularized with no need for God at all. These themes became popular in the media. Instead of popes and bishops doing the thinking for you, it was now the new psychologists, the new sociologists, the new music, the new movies, the new cultural icons, all seductively calling you to embrace the Zeitgeist. Uncritical acceptance of these often unreliable elements meant that the old forms of anti-intellectualism were being replaced by new forms of anti-intellectualism.

America has always been a pragmatic place, a country of doers, not thinkers. Horatio Alger without any education pulled himself up by his own bootstraps. The successful businessman with no formal education was lionized. Teddy Roosevelt said it was better to make history than to write it. Henry Ford thought history was "bunk." Advertising surely tries to do our thinking for us. Widely read publications such as *Vogue, People, Seventeen*, the *New York Times, The Village Voice* impact the thoughts of readers.

STEPS TOWARD A BETTER SPIRITUALITY

One of the first steps to take in the search for a better spirituality is to look critically at the human sciences, accept what is good, dismiss what is not helpful, and rediscover learning. Part of learning is openness to the new and remembering the lessons of the past. One of these lessons is to beware of false teachers, as St. Paul said so frequently. They are here in our midst as well.

Church history teaches us important lessons in which to find comfort and courage. How many times in the church's long history were reforms necessary to return the church to its mission of preaching the gospel? In the past bishops were removed for malfeasance of office, especially for simony. It was not easy then and it is not easy now.

Here is one lesson from World War II. At the end of the war, Angelo Giuseppe Roncalli, the future John XXIII, was sent by Pope Pius XII from his diplomatic post in Turkey to be the papal nuncio in France. One of his jobs was to remove from office (via resignation) three pro-Nazi bishops and secure elevation to cardinal of three French archbishops who "had opposed Nazism and any form of collaboration."[6]

Another lesson from history takes us back to the famous church historian John Tracey Ellis, who in 1955 openly criticized the anti-intellectualism of American Catholic universities.[7]

Popular culture and larger society want one to believe that we live in a two-story house with religion in the upper story, a matter of personal preference and subjective belief. *(What is true for you may not be true for me.)* The main floor of the house is home to the secular sciences uncritically accepted as objective truth. Some suggest a Christian worldview has to move downstairs to the main floor and make its impact felt there too, especially in areas praised by Vatican II. Rediscovering learning is as important today as it was in the sixteenth-century Council of Trent.

Cardinal Dulles rightly says, "Religious illiteracy has sunk to a new low. We are in urgent need of far-reaching intellectual, spiritual and moral regeneration."[8] Yet our anti-intellectual environment keeps tempting us to avoid this work.

Bernard Lonergan sums it all up in this way:

> Many among you will find this picture too bleak…the crisis then, that I have been attempting to depict is a crisis not of faith but of culture. There has been no new revelation from on high to replace the revelation given through Christ Jesus. There has been written no new Bible and there has been founded no new Church to link us with Him….There is bound to be a solid right that is determined to live in a world that no longer exists. There is bound to be formed a scattered left, captured by now this, now that new development, exploring now this and now that new possibility. But what will count is perhaps a less populated center, big enough to be at home in both the old and the new, painstaking enough to work out one by one the transitions to be made, strong enough to refuse half-measures and insist on complete solutions even though it has to wait.[9]

RELIGIOUS AND SECULAR ILLITERACY

The root of much traditional anti-intellectualism is loss of our native sense of wonder, with the subsequent rise of intellectual laziness. It starts with what Cardinal Avery Dulles calls religious illiteracy. What is religious illiteracy? We may reverently recite the creed while not wondering about its beauty. The sacraments may be rightly administered without appreciating their luster. One may follow the Beatitudes and vigorously pursue peace and social justice and lack any insight into the beauty of what is going forward. Perhaps Augustine's words have been forgotten: "Late have I loved thee, oh beauty, so ancient and so new. Late have I loved thee."[10]

It is not just religious illiteracy but secular illiteracy as well. Some conservative religious leaders believe that the faith of their people will not be helped by secular wisdom and may even be harmed. This forces people of faith to live on the second floor and makes them vulnerable to attack by some antireligious forces living on the first floor.

Marco Polo courted trouble by learning new ideas in his travels to China in the thirteenth century. Even on his deathbed when told to recant, his reply was: I never told the half of it. Galileo risked his life by looking into a telescope and so did Copernicus and Kepler. Darwin became the darling of the London social set by going to the Galapagos Islands. Freud's journey into the self-conscious was thought mischievous at best. B. F. Skinner defied academia by insisting all of a person's behavior is determined only by his reinforcement history (rewards and punishments). The message in former times was *"to steer clear of these individuals. You could lose your faith."*

This fear of learning what people are saying is really a lack of faith *in faith itself*. Resistance to learning often results in a siege mentality; your eyes are closed to new insights. But even if you close your eyes, that will not destroy the sun. Christianity exists for mankind. Walls should not be constructed around the spirituality of humility, kindness, and sympathy.

The temptation in the Garden of Eden was not the temptation to become educated or learned. It was not as if Adam and Eve would sin if they studied psychology or church history. The temptation was to self-absorption and not to self-learning. They would sin if they made themselves the center of things.

The temptation was to self-worship, ignoring our Creator, and setting up our own definition of good and evil, which is self-worship, indeed. The temptation was to believe the serpent's lie: If we experience evil, we will really be free like God.

THE LIES OF ANTI-INTELLECTUALISM

The root of the anti-intellectualism of those who consider themselves progressive is the fear of missing out and fascination with being in the vanguard. It is the fear of being considered "out of touch," "not with it." the fear of missing something important, the fear of rejection, of not being accepted by those who count.

Just as Adam and Eve were lied to in the Garden of Eden, many of us may be tempted by a couple of Satan's lies in the contemporary world. The first says: *Be cynical about learning*. There is always some truth in every lie. The truth here is that the learned have not displayed untarnished ideals on which we can anchor firm hope. A thief with a lamp can steal more than a thief without a lamp.

The second lie is: *It does not matter anyway because the church is run on power and money and nothing else*. The truth in this lie is that some in power can do almost anything they like and no one is there to stop them.

The goal of these two lies is universal disillusionment with church institutions. These lies tell us not to try. For the devil knows all that is necessary for the triumph of evil is that we do nothing.

But these lies are so widespread in the media: Be entertained and let us do the thinking for you. So many have matriculated from institutions of higher learning that no longer believe in higher learning. Graduates seem to depart universities without any excitement for a life of learning.

This is particularly problematic in this first decade of the twenty-first century when the church in America is so troubled. It is time to rediscover learning. There is so much new to be learned about how we are to renew ourselves and our church and so little motivation to do so. A person who is not motivated to learn finds his or her spiritual life atrophied and stunted.

The thirteenth century is often called the greatest of centuries because of the magnificent saints whom God raised up at that time. But as Henri Daniel-Rops points out, the counterpoint is illustrated by a speech given in 1245 at Lyon by Pope Innocent IV: "The abominable morals of prelates and faithful, the insolence of the Saracens, the schism of the Greeks, the brutality of the Tartars, the persecutions by an impious emperor…such are the five wounds of which the Church is dying."[11]

One needs to understand the story Jesus told of the sower who sowed good seed in his field, and while asleep his enemy came and sowed weeds among the wheat.

That is why the church is always in need of reform, for the Lord gives us the truth, the beauty, and the goodness of salvation and we poor sinful mortals obscure it in so many ways. We carry these great gifts in earthen vessels, so purification is required to make sure that people have ears to hear the good news with the grace of God.

THE NEED FOR REFORM AND RENEWAL

Purification and renewal of the church are necessary so it can more clearly be seen to be what Christ has made it to be, namely, the community of salvation through word and sacrament.

A good example of this "let us do your thinking for you" style is a text in European history used in our Boys Town High School. The chapter on sixteenth-century Europe focuses on the great Protestant reformers such as Luther, Calvin, and Melancthon. The basic message is that the church of Rome at the time was filled with corrupt practices and that the reformers themselves were equally filled with extremists views. The authors seemed to want students to embrace the conclusion that both Roman Catholics and Protestants are guilty of perverse views, so we need to avoid Christianity altogether. This politically correct textbook is such poor scholarship, but it gives us the opportunity to teach our kids important lessons. Yes, there were immoral popes and bishops in the Middle Ages and they gave very bad examples and the church needed to be purged of them.

These bad shepherds, I told my students, must hear the words of St. Augustine: "Even the strong sheep, if he turns his eye away from the Lord's laws and looks at the man set over him, notices when his shepherd is living wickedly and begins to say in his heart: if my pastor lives like that, why should I not live like him."[12]

This is a great opportunity for kids to understand that the high school history text compared the *ideals* of the author's position with the *bad practices* of some Christians of the sixteenth century. It is a cheap trick to compare your *ideals* with their *practices*. You need to compare your ideals with their ideals, or your practices with theirs. Anything else is unfair. If the fires of devotion burn low, the remedy is not to learn to live in the cold, but rather to reinkindle those fires of devotion. Learning this is a way to help young people not fall for such cheap tricks.

Your help in the reform and renewal of the church is needed. You will feel so much better about your role if you discover your learning potential. There is a whole lot of denial going on in the rejection of learning.

Once again Henri Daniel-Rops offers an important insight when writing about tenth-century Christianity: "Spiritual progress is never set on foot once and for all. There must be a constant struggle with the forces of darkness, against the weakness of the human heart so prone to compromise. Reform is a continual necessity, and the Church understood this as much in the 10th Century as she had done in the days of St. Columbanus and St. Boniface."[13]

Thomas Aquinas wrote in the thirteenth century: "To be a glorious Church not having spot or wrinkle is the ultimate end to which we are brought by the Passion of Christ. Hence this will be in heaven and not on earth."[14]

In calling the Second Vatican Council, Pope John XXIII wrote:

> "[T]here will be one fold and one shepherd" (John 10:16). This irresistible assurance was the compelling motive which led Us to announce publicly our resolve to call an Ecumenical Council. Bishops will come together there from every corner of the world to discuss important matters of religion. But

the most pressing topics will be those which concern the spread of the Catholic faith, *the revival of Christian standards of morality,* and the bringing of ecclesiastical discipline into closer accord with the needs and conditions of our times. This in itself will provide an outstanding example of truth, unity and love. May those who are separated from this Apostolic See, beholding this manifestation of unity, derive from it the inspiration to seek out that unity which Jesus Christ prayed for so ardently from his heavenly Father.[15]

The Constitution on the Church says it well: "The Church, embracing sinners in her bosom, is at the same time holy and always in need of being purified, and incessantly pursues the path of penance and renewal."[16]

The church recognized in Vatican II's *Gaudium et spes* the "signs of the times," which placed an emphasis on seeing the optimistic aspects of modern human progress. Many theologians, including Karl Rahner and Hans Urs von Balthasar, were unhappy with *Gaudium et spes,* pointing out how its incarnational theology failed to give precedence to the central acts of redemption, namely, the cross and resurrection, and our chance to share in them. Looking back some four decades later, their criticism seems more than justified.

SOME STEPS TO CONSIDER

Finally, there are some basic guidelines for rediscovering learning and bringing the life of the intellect to bear on our spiritual growth and on renewal and purification of the church. Various new resources are available today that were not before.

Consider starting with *four projects* either individually or as a group.

The first is the scriptures. Read the gospels and Paul's Letter to the Romans. What better place than to be nourished than by God's word. *Barclay's Commentary* is widely used and easily understood. Craig Evans's *Fabricating Jesus*, written in 2006, is a powerful resource.

The second is history, especially church history. One of the best ways to motivate yourself to study church history is to realize what help it will give you in your spiritual life and in the reform of the church. Why? Because through the centuries the church has experienced troubles as great as our own; by studying that history we gain insight and motivation regarding what is to be done. Henri Daniel-Rops is a fine place to start.

The third is the *Catechism of the Catholic Church*. Here you will find riches galore in words not too difficult to understand, words that inspire as well as illuminate.

The fourth is to start developing the habit of critical thinking. When you hear of some historian or psychologist or sociologist announcing a novel theory or procedure, ask yourself, "What are the main criticisms of this view?" It will help you separate the wheat from the chaff. You do this regularly with papal encyclicals. Why not do the same with secular pronouncements?

Finally there are three important rules to remember:

1. *Learn good study habits.* Find a mentor who can help you with that as well and remember that studying will get easier as you go along.
2. *Take what you have learned to prayer.* Thank the Lord for

the gift of your mind as well as your heart and soul. Thank the Lord that your Christian tradition has always held that faith and science, although not the same, are friends and complement each other. The public prayer of the church is very helpful in this regard.

3. *Do things gradually*. Go slowly and, if you cannot do everything, do something. Start reading your Bible every day, even just for a few minutes, for that is a great beginning. Learn from the mistakes of others; you will not live long enough to make all of them yourself.

Bernard Lonergan writes:

> Classical culture has given way to a modern culture and, I would submit, the crisis of our age is in no small measure the fact that the modern culture has not yet reached its maturity. The classical mediation of meaning has broken down; the breakdown has been affected by a whole array of new and more effective techniques; but their very multiplicity and complexity leave us bewildered, disoriented, confused, preyed upon by anxiety, dreading lest we fall victims to the up-to-date myth of ideology and the hypnotic, highly effective magic of thought control.[17]

Lonergan leaves us with this concluding thought:

> Ours is a new age, and enormous tasks lie ahead. We shall be all the more likely to surmount them, if we take the trouble to understand what is going forward and why.[18]

Let us be patient, but let us begin now.

148

Chapter 9
POLITICAL CORRECTNESS

Political correctness is the seventh secular challenge to consider. In popular jargon, it is taking your cues from the headliners by being trendy, up-to-date, attuned to the times, and worthy of praise from these cultural trendsetters. It is also fear of being left out. Political correctness differs from being stylish or following the fads in the clothing industry. It is different from the social norms of society, which involve customs and mores. European society is different from African society. The difference is not about political correctness. New England hospitality is different from Southern hospitality and that is not about political correctness.

INITIAL CONSIDERATIONS

Political correctness has to do with the politics of movements that set a new standard to be imposed on others by what is often perceived as an elite group. It usually insists on "forced conformity" for the sake of conformity. Even when the movement is a good one, forced conformity sometimes means doing the right thing for the wrong reason. Those who keep to the standard are praised. Those who do not are shunned.

Political correctness has been around for centuries. What is new in this postmodern age is the use of superso-phisticated tools of social manipulation to help people grad-ually change their view, often without their being conscious of these efforts of social manipulation.

The Vatican II document, *The Church in the Modern World*, told us all to attend to the human sciences such as sociology and psychology. For years working at Boys Town, I knew how marketing used these social sciences in a clever fashion to persuade children to buy toys, games, clothes, cereal, and a consumer view of life, but I really was unaware of how marketing had become so powerful in this postmod-ern world, purposefully conditioning even mature adults to arrive at not their own conclusions, but the marketers' desired conclusions. As Gene Veith Jr. said regarding market-ing for purposes of political correctness: "Truth is not the issue. The issue is power."[1] That is an earthquake in itself. Vatican II reminded us to look at the signs of the times. The times have changed so greatly that the world is now post-modern.

In the aftermath of World War II, George Orwell wrote a classic book entitled *1984*. The whole world had just expe-rienced a life-and-death struggle with totalitarian regimes stamping out individual freedom and demanding not only external conformity, but also internal conviction from all peoples under their control.

It is a chilling novel telling the story of one man's strug-gle to hold onto his individual identity, his inner worth, and what John Paul II would later refer to as the dignity of the human person. In the end, he fails, succumbing to what Orwell calls the "Thought Police."

Political correctness of the new postmodern culture has morphed into a frightening phenomenon eerily similar to Orwell's Thought Police.

To understand this growing phenomenon, let us unpack the issue first by describing what is so different about the postmodern world, and secondly, how does slick marketing work in this new context?

POSTMODERN WORLD CHARACTERISTICS

Many contemporary commentators now describe today's world as *postmodern*. In so many ways, it is different from the modern world. It is commonplace among commentators to attribute three basic characteristics to this postmodern world.

First, in this brave new world, there seems to be no objective truth.[2] Truth, strange to say, has moved from the intellect to the will. In the modern world, there was objective truth. In that world, you might argue about what was objectively true, but there was agreement about its existence. One could argue that there really was a God as the Christians and Jews and Muslims claimed, or argue that this God was only a fantasy as Karl Marx and Sigmund Freud held.

Today truth is a matter of personal choice or preference. If you like the idea of God, good. If you think it is cool not to embrace the idea of God, that is fine, too. The shift to personal preference is momentous. So we still talk about truths, but what is truth for you may not be truth for me. And that is cool. Truth is now in the will.

Secondly, in this postmodern world, many hold that moral values are relative.[3] There are no moral absolutes. Moral values have also moved from the intellect to the will and are now basically a matter of preference. If you like the idea of the Ten Commandments, good for you. If you don't like the idea, that is cool, too. Postmodern people are comfortable saying, "I like the idea of seeking international justice and fairness" or "I don't like the idea." In this world, Hans Urs von Balthasar's theological aesthetic can be very attractive as long as everyone understands that it is a matter of choice, not a matter of a reasonable conclusion or revelation. Where the modern world tried to rule out religion, the postmodern world does not. Moral theologians such as Charles Curran and Richard McCormick are perceived as arguing for no moral absolutes in the modern culture of their times. It means something entirely different in a postmodern culture.

Something else is going on here. As Gene Veith notes: "The only consistent position for postmodernists is that all talk of morality, *including their own*, only masks the will to power.... I must have the power to do what I want and you do not have the power to stop me."[4]

The third characteristic of postmodern world is insistence on the social construction of reality by lots of different communities.[5] If you are, for example, a white male, your status in society is determined not by your individual responsibility, but by the fact that you are a white male. You should very much feel collective guilt for all the horrible things the white race has done to others through hundreds and hundreds of years. If you are a female, your status in society is established by the fact that you are a female, with oppression of females common to all cultures. You should feel oppressed.

Woe be it to you if you claim that moral values are not simply relative to a person's desires, but are the objective ordinances of the God who made the heavens and the earth.

Woe to you who say the individual is responsible for his or her actions. In this culture, individuals cannot be blamed. It is the community to which one belongs that determines that identity.

In the modern culture, the ecumenical movement was not as much a success as many hoped. The postmodern impulse now is to go beyond ecumenism to the interfaith arena and to say all the great religions of the world are valid for the people who want them to be valid.[6]

MARKETING AND ITS EFFECTS

This is an age of marketing. How does marketing fit in to the postmodern world? It is the main engine that propels the culture forward via political correctness. Before we see how this works, let us recall that in postmodern Europe, forces are at work to drive traditional or orthodox Christianity completely out of public life. How about here in America?

Let us listen to Tammy Bruce. She is a strident feminist, the former president of the Los Angeles chapter of the National Organization of Women (NOW), who has become a best-selling author and syndicated talk-show host. This activist is a credible voice with solid liberal credentials, yet she is considered a traitor by many postmodern activists because she exposes what she calls the new Thought Police of our times. Somewhat ironically, she is a good friend of Dr. Laura, although they are at opposite ends of so many issues. Bruce says, "Christianity represents to the Left (in America) the principal threat to their hollow, empty agenda."[7] Then she adds, "The ultimate goal of the liberal elite has never been to *change* the Catholic Church. It has been to *destroy* it."[8]

It seems that this argument about political correctness articulated by Bruce and others means that Christianity is not something to be reformed or updated or renewed. It is simply to be totally eliminated.

This attitude has been reflected in some recent artistic expressions that are sacrilegious and offensive to Christian believers. In 1999, the Brooklyn Museum of Art displayed a work entitled *The Holy Virgin Mary* that depicted elephant dung on the image of Mary surrounded by pornographic magazine pictures of female genitalia . When people said it was very offensive bigotry, the response was to take refuge in a new notion of art. The postmodern strategy is to change the meaning of things, in this case, art. The artist said there was absolutely nothing wrong with his Mary picture, because it was a positive religious symbol misunderstood. For example, Edward Rothstein in the *New York Times* said that there was no problem at all with the artist's work. What was at stake was a "Philistine misunderstanding of the art by its religious opponents."[9]

Similar tactics were used in a recent Madonna concert in which the performer arose on a stage fastened to a mirrored cross, wearing a false crown of thorns. In this postmodern world, multiculturalism is used as a marketing ploy to sell this relativism.

Many argue the postmodern world feels the need to do away with that type of Christianity which says there are moral absolutes, things that we should not do, and things that are never permitted and should not be engaged in.

How does marketing fit in? The marketing goal is to have us change our minds in a slick fashion with or without our realizing this has been done to us. This is also perhaps a new thought for my readers. You have to see how powerful these marketing tools are. Is this a major challenge in our world or something we need not worry about? You have to decide. The sixth edition of Terence A. Shimp's *Advertising, Promotion & Supplemental Aspects of Integrated Marketing Communications* describes these methods in detail.[10] Shimp gives a good description of the highly acclaimed Elaboration Likelihood Model.[11] It is an eye-opener.

Pratkanis and Aronson describe this approach as pre-persuasion.[12] For example, compassion is a highly regarded feeling in our culture. Whatever you are selling, make sure it is compassionate and the opposite of it is lacking in compassion.

There are four P's in marketing:

- **product**
- **price**
- **place**
- **promotion**

Persuasion touches each of them. What the postmodern world is selling is a worldview, a new way of seeing and doing, not selling a Lexus or a computer, but the marketing methods are the same. Each of the four P's has to be revised. The product has to be repackaged. The pricing has to be different, just as place and promotion do. This can be cleverly done when it comes to religion or other major issues.

THREE PHASES OF CONSCIOUS MANIPULATION

The point to remember here is that this is *conscious manipulation* of people and it usually comes in three phases.

The first phase is *desensitization*, which can be described as a continuous flood of postmodern advertising presented in the least offensive fashion possible.[13] A marketer will say, for example, "Let us present to the Christian community the idea that all religions are good as long as they make people happy." Then, in order to desensitize Christians, show Buddhists, Hindus, and New Age gurus capable of "channeling" ancient Phoenician warriors or extraterrestrial life forms as really nice people whom you would not mind having as neighbors. Show Scientologists, who believe in communication from outer space, as happy, productive people. Present those who think Jesus Christ is a very nice person—who did not die for us—as good folks. In other words, desensitize loyal Christians and, with clever marketing, help them to begin thinking these folks merit no more than a shrug of the shoulders. When this happens, your battle for postmodern religion is off to a good start, and Christianity as we know it is on the way to the recycling plant.

Michael Warren says, "It is not overt coercion. It is one group's covert orchestration of compliance by another group's restructuring of the consciousness of the second group."[14]

In this desensitization phase, you see news clips about these folks helping the community and suggesting that there are so many of them and they are all real nice people. The goal is to have your Christian people no longer look askance at folks identified as Wiccan or demon worshippers.

The second phase is called *jamming*, which makes use of associative conditioning and direct emotional modeling.[15] In this jamming or scare phase, it is important to bash anyone who opposes your postmodern agenda. Anyone who claims there are moral absolutes should be shouted down or laughed to scorn. Publicly ridicule them. Get scripture scholars to say the scriptures do not support the traditional view of moral absolutes. The key is autosuggestion: If I don't go along, I will be rejected and made fun of. Clergy need very much to be liked by all and are thus particularly susceptible to the threat of being shouted down or laughed at publicly.

The third phase is *conversion*, which Kirk and Madsen call "conversion of the average American's emotions, mind and will through a planned psychological attack, in the form of propaganda fed to the nation via the media."[16] So now you say that Christianity is true for you personally, that moral rules are relative; you should accept those rules you like and reject those you do not feel comfortable with.

Tammy Bruce says, "Thirty years ago, black, feminist and gay civil-rights organizations were groups that a classical liberal could be proud to be associated with. Not any longer."[17] Could she be right? What does she mean? There are some leaders in each of these organizations making it their business to try to shame into silence anyone who disagrees with them.

There is nothing new about thought control or free-speech opponents, but in the past, they have mostly been identified with either conservative religious movements or right-wing political movements.

Tammy Bruce is saying, "From my vantage point on the Left, I have seen the new version of Orwell's Thought Police emerge under the guise of improving the quality of life."[18] She seems to be on to something very, very important. Or is she greatly deceived herself?

She is particularly incensed about the promoters of progress insisting that others who disagree with them be silenced, using the marketing techniques described above. She says they are making the same mistake that the Vietnam War strategists made with the belief that "to save a village, they need to destroy it." The Founding Fathers of this country believed in John Locke's ideal of classical liberalism, namely, as much freedom as possible and as little restriction as necessary. The postmodern world rejects this.

The political correctness described here can become a new Inquisition, run by stern, unbending marketers. Is this an exaggeration? That is a very important question to ask. In AA circles, it is commonplace to describe enforced silence and enforced family taboos on discussing alcoholism with the analogy of an elephant in the living room. The elephant is there, but nobody mentions it. Everyone knows it is there. It is clearly controlling so much, but no one speaks of it.

Are there parishes and dioceses that have an elephant in the room? Perhaps yes, perhaps no. It is a question worth asking. Enforced silence today comes as easily from the Left as it has in the past from the Right.

In the twentieth century, we first lived in the age of monarchies (World War I), followed by the age of totalitarianism (World War II). Then came the atomic age and the cold war. This was followed by our current age of marketing and globalization, which now holds center stage.

SOME WAYS TO RESPOND POSITIVELY TO THE CHALLENGES OF POLITICAL CORRECTNESS

- We need to wake up, be attentive, and realize there is an agenda afoot that tries to dupe, deceive, and manipulate. When that lightbulb goes on in our heads, we now have in our grasp the ability, if we so choose, to mitigate and critically respond to the persuasive powers of mass communication in this age. Knowing the agenda puts power in your hands.

- We need to turn on its head their view that truth is not so important and what is important is power. We need to insist that the issue is truth and not power. Environmental conditioning is an instrument to gain power. It has nothing to do with truth and charity.

- We need to please everyone (especially the new Thought Police) is not a mandate found in the gospels. Fear of being shouted down and rejected needs to be subdued. Jesus did not say that God is love at the expense of truth or moral goodness or beauty. To separate one of these is to distort the good news.

- We need to realize with the famous French patristic scholar, Jean Danielou, that the truth is never popular. He calls it the scandal of truth.[19] On the other hand, Jesus tells his followers in John's Gospel that "the truth will make you free"(8:32). In every age, from the early Christian martyrs to our own time, truth has worn a crown of thorns.

- For those who feel duped and manipulated by being intentionally conditioned to arrive at conclusions they think are their own, it is good to remember that the remedy for mistaking thinking and believing is not to give up thinking or believing, but to develop better controls over them.

If there is any sense to what is being written about now, then it may be that Vatican II's *Church in the Modern World* now needs to be supplemented with a new document written by the bishops and Holy Father entitled *The Church in the Postmodern World*.

EPILOGUE

As a youngster, I often wished there was a guide for the road that lay ahead. I was entering the Lord's service in 1954 and what was needed was a trusted guide. When setting out from St. Louis in 1803, Lewis and Clark found a trusted guide, Sacagawea, as the long boat moved through upper reaches of the Missouri River to explore the Louisiana Purchase. Dante had Virgil and Beatrice as his guides for the journey through *The Divine Comedy*. Athena and Mercury guided her son, Aeneas, from Troy to Livonia in the *Aeneid*.

There was no such guide for my own journey. However, there was an excellent mentor during my studies in Rome, and to this day I am grateful to him.

I felt like Frodo in *The Fellowship of the Ring*. The characters have discovered the source of the power of the rings. Gathered in council, the decision is made that someone must travel to the mountain of Sauron and throw the ring into the fire. There is much debating as to how this feat will be accomplished and who could carry it out successfully. This brings the good leader, Elrond, to address the council:

> "The road must be trod, but it will be very hard. And neither strength nor wisdom will carry us far upon it. This quest may be attempted by the weak with as much hope as the strong. Yet such is oft by the course of deeds that move the wheels of the world: small hands do them because they must, while the eyes of the great are elsewhere."[1]

I knew the Lord sent me on a journey just as he sends everyone who comes into the world.

What you have just read is a guidebook for a very troubled time. It does not tell everything, but it contains many of the secrets of a successful journey: seven crucial areas where the postmodern world has not enriched, but has challenged, our spiritual lives, and successful strategies to overcome these secular challenges. In more than four decades of this journey, I have seen many lose their way in these areas and have tried to learn from them.

I was at the Second Vatican Council working on the floor every day in the third and fourth sessions while doing doctoral studies at the same time. Blessed Pope John XXIII had said it was to be a pastoral council. I was hoping it would give to the church the six pastoral things that Martin Luther had cried out for in the sixteenth century. None of them touched the creed and none of them were contrary to the gospels. We got five: the vernacular in the liturgy, the communion cup, lay ministers, communion in the hand, scripture renewal.

I saw so many people make so many mistakes following the Zeitgeist uncritically while Vatican II was being implemented. Here in America the implementation of the Vatican II decrees was, to use a phrase made famous by John J. Hughes, carried out in large part in an adolescent fashion due to the adolescent culture of the 1960s and 70s. Like a child entering his teenage years, priests stood in the pulpit and laughed to scorn beloved practices of their childhood such as the Latin Mass, fasting, novenas, forty hours adoration, the rosary, holy water, the *Dies Irae,* and our somber funerals. More importantly, like a fourteen-year-old boy who heretofore thought his dad a wonder-worker and now turns on him, in public and in private, they made the Holy Father and what he taught the object of ridicule.

Many of our priests, bishops, and theologians, as well as religious women, were quite unprepared to lead in this time of change, not possessing the special skills that such a time requires. Pope John XXIII often said we needed to enrich the old with the new, but few in America knew how to do this. Too many priests, bishops, and theologians, through no fault of their own, confused Pope John's call to read the signs of the times with uncritical acceptance of the values of our culture. So many of the mainline Protestant churches had abandoned restraint and we were in ecumenical dialogue with them. The vast majority of Catholic laity still cherished their faith and still practiced it faithfully, while harboring serious doubts about who was really in charge: those who thought the Age of Aquarius had begun or those who held firm to Cardinal Ottaviani's motto, *"Idem semper"* (Always the same). I learned a lot of lessons there. I read the signs of the times and saw the potential of this age for good and for evil. There are secular challenges in all cultures and ours is no exception.

After Vatican II we were all repeatedly being exhorted to join one of two Catholic camps, both grabbing media attention: the progressives, too many of whom, to say it charitably, to an extent embraced the culture blindly, and the conservatives, too many of whom, to put it mildly, almost rejected all its values except the old status quo, traditional ecclesiastical power, and wealth management. And each had their own multifaceted agenda.

The question I kept asking myself was why I was so unhappy with both of these agendas. It gradually became clear from working with America's "throwaway children" that the gospel was not sufficiently shaping the culture (like leaven in the dough) but in some cases vice versa. It was clear that the church in America needed to get beyond its own adolescence of uncritical acceptance and embark on deeper purification and more authentic renewal.

I lived through the huge controversy over birth control starting in the summer of 1968. So many liberals and conservatives buying into cultural ideology seemed almost to elevate it to the single most important facet of American church life, much to the neglect of the gospel. It seemed to me that both sides were nearly ready to die on a hill that was not Calvary.

I lived through the Vietnam War and tried to learn its lessons. Too many on both sides rejected the middle ground. The good leader Elrond was right: "The road must be trod, but it will be very hard."

More than anywhere else I have learned the lessons of the long spiritual journey from my twenty-three years here at Boys Town. I have seen thousands and thousands of young people come to us, all of them filled with anger, loneliness, frustration, and loss of hope, living in a postmodern culture: antiauthoritarian and cynical. They feel free to experience everything. They embrace MTV's ideology. In some ways, they are helpless victims. These lives are reduced to a single narrow focus: Should I destroy my life (drugs, sex, and alcohol) or go on. Is it worth the effort to swim against the tide of pain and despair, alienation and dysfunctionality? Or shall I curse God and die? Because of their past, they believe that love (even God's love) has to be merited and they are convinced they are unworthy. This is the lie Adam and Eve believed when they hid themselves from God in the garden. Our job is to help them choose life.

And finally, there came upon us the recent terrible troubles in the American church, scandals of enormous proportion, tragedies that will be with us for the rest of our lives.

Just as forty years ago Vatican II was a time for self-purification and renewal in the universal church, so, too, now is the time for reform and renewal in the American church. Pope Benedict is wise to look at Vatican II again and see where we have gone astray.

All of us have the opportunity to make a difference. We have the chance to renew ourselves and our church as St. Francis did in his day, as St. Dominic did for his time, as St. Catherine of Siena did, and as the great saints Charles Borromeo, Ignatius of Loyola, and Francis Xavier did in the Reformation.

To do so we need to begin with our own spiritual lives. *"Ecclesia semper reformanda est."* The church must always be purified and reformed, and the purification and reformation start with you and me. Let us begin.

It is my hope these thoughts have been helpful to you as a guidebook in "following the Lord" through troubled times.

Take what you find useful and leave the rest behind. Above all, let the thoughts here challenge your own current *behaviors,* not just your thoughts or feelings. Why? Because a guidebook is about behavior—going to important places and doing God-centered things.

It is a journey, a pilgrimage. If all you do is move from helpless and cynical behavior to hopeful behavior, then the journey will have been well worth the effort. It is a great world. Let us make it better.

NOTES

Introduction

1. St. Augustine, *Retractationes,* trans. Sister Mary Inez Bogan (Washington: Catholic University of America Press, 1968), 156.

2. St. Gregory the Great, *Regula Pastoralis,* trans. Henry David, SJ (Westminster, MD: The Newman Press, 1950), 35.

3. Ibid., 24

4. St. Thomas Aquinas, *S.T.,* III, q.8, art.3, ad. 2.

5. Medard Kehland and Werner Loser, *The Von Balthasar Reader* (New York: Crossroads, 1982), 261–62.

Chapter 1

1. Numerous books and articles have chronicled this story. We are using Dana Mack's well-known *The Assault on Parenthood* (New York: Simon & Schuster, 1997), Christopher Lasch, *The Culture of Narcissism* (New York: Norton, 1978), as well as Joyce Milton, *The Road to Malpsychia: Humanistic Psychology and Our Discontents* (San Francisco: Encounter Books, 2002). Many of our citations come from these and other sources. What is new is not recitation of the facts, but connecting this story to the loss of authority among church leaders through a silo effect. (See page 28 for a definition of the phrase silo effect.)

2. Benjamin Spock, *Baby and Child Care* (London: Star Books, 1983), 12–18.

3. Haim Ginott, *Between Parent and Child* (New York: MacMillan, 1965).

4. Haim Ginott, *Between Parent and Teenager* (New York: Macmillan, 1969).

5. Thomas Gordon, *P.E.T. Parent Effectiveness Training* (New York: Penguin, 1970).

6. Rudolf Dreikurs, *The Challenge of Parenthood* (New York: Penguin, 1992), 17–18.

7. Dana Mack, *The Assault on Parenthood* (New York: Simon and Schuster, 1997).

8. Lee and Marlene Canter, *Assertive Discipline for Parents* (New York: Harper and Row, 1988), 4.

9. Alice Miller, *For Your Own Good: Hidden Cruelty in Child-Rearing and the Roots of Violence.* (New York: Noonday Press, 1983), 147–80.

10. Alice Miller, *Drama of the Gifted Child: The Search for the True Self,* (New York: Basic Books, 1994), 88–89.

11. John Bradshaw, *Bradshaw on: The Family* (Deerfield Beach, FL: Health Communications, 1988), 18–21.

12. Daniel Yankelovich, *New Rules* (New York: Random House, 1981). Also Whitney Missildine, *Your Inner Child of the Past* (New York: Simon and Schuster, 1993).

13. Carl Rogers, *On Becoming a Person* (Boston: Houghton Mifflin, 1961).

14. Carl Rogers, "Speaking Personally," in the *Carl Rogers Reader,* ed. Howard Kirschenbaum and Valerie Land Henderson (Boston: Houghton Mifflin, 1989), 48–49.

15. Peter D. Kramer, *Listening to Prozac: A Psychiatrist Explores Anti-Depressant Drugs and the Making of the Self* (New York: Viking, 1993), 222.

16. Abraham Maslow, *Toward a Psychology of Being* (New York: Van Nostrand Reinhold, 1968).

17. *Journals of Abraham Maslow,* vol. 1, cited in Joyce Milton, *The Road to Malpsychia: Humanistic Psychology and our Discontents* (San Francisco: Encounter Books, 2002), 139.

18. Timothy Leary, *Flashbacks: A Personal and Cultural History of an Era* (New York: Putnam, 1981).

19. Bernard Lonergan, *Method in Theology* (New York: Herder and Herder, 1972), 57–58. See also Matthew Lamb, ed., *Creativity and Method, Essays in Honor of Bernard Lonergan* (Milwaukee: Marquette University Press, 1981).

20. Mack, *Assault on Parenthood*, 34.

21. Ibid. The unhappiness of the vast majority of Americans with our schools can be traced to a similar anti-authoritarian onslaught of educational experts. See for example a survey by Paul A. Zoch, *Doomed to Fail* (Chicago: Ivan R. Dee Publisher, 2004) as well as Robert J. Marzano, *What Works in Schools* (Alexandria, VA: Association for Supervision and Curriculum Development, 2003).

22. Father Sigismund Brettle, cited in Anonymous, *The Persecution of the Catholic Church in the Third Reich* (Fort Collins, CO: Roger McCaffrey Publishing, originally published in 1941), 62.

23. Cited in Ragan Sutterfield, "No Easy Saint: Bonhoeffer and Just War," *Books and Culture* 11 (May–June 2005): 34. Also Stanley Hauerwas, *Performing the Faith: Bonhoeffer and the Practice of Nonviolence* (Grand Rapids, MI: Brozos Press, 2004).

24. Karl Menninger, *Whatever Became of Sin* (New York: Hawthorn Books, 1973).

25. Robert Schuller, *Self-Esteem: The New Reformation* (Nashville: Thomas Nelson, 1982).

26. Bernard Lonergan, "Dialectic of Authority," in *The Lonergan Reader*, ed. Mark Morelli and Elizabeth Morelli (Toronto: University of Toronto Press, 1997), 55.

27. Cardinal Avery Dulles, "True and False Reform," *First Things* 135 (August–September, 2003): 18.

28. Paul Vitz, "Support from Psychology for the Fatherhood of God," *Homiletic and Pastoral Review* 97 (February 1997): 7–19. See also Paul Vitz, *Faith of the Fatherless* (Dallas: Spence, 1999).

Chapter 2

1. Harvey Cox, *The Secular City* (New York: Macmillan, 1965).

2. Herbert Haag, *Is Original Sin in Scripture?* trans. Dorothy Thompson (New York: Sheed and Ward, 1969).

3. Ibid., 106–7.

4. For a stimulating discussion of this issue, see Nancy Pearcy, *Total Truth: Liberating Christianity from Its Cultural Captivity* (Wheaton, IL: Crossway Books, 2004), 47–62.

5. Sean Fagan, SM, *Has Sin Changed?* (Wilmington, DE: Michael Glazier, 1977).

6. Ibid., 57.

7. Ibid., 68.

8. Ibid., 74.

9. Ibid., 128.

10. Ibid., 3.

11. Bernard Lonergan, *Method in Theology* (New York: Herder and Herder, 1972), 364.

12. *Catechism of the Catholic Church* (Chicago: Loyola University Press, 1994), 418.

13. Ibid., 421.

14. Ibid., 418.

15. Margaret O'Brien Steinfels, quoted in *Catholic Eye*, 197 (June 30, 2002): 1.

16. Henri de Lubac, *Further Paradoxes* (Westminster, MD: Newman Press, 1958), 126–27.

17. Cardinal Avery Dulles, "True and False Reform," *First Things* 135 (August–September 2003): 25.

18. Ken Woodward, "The Last Respectable Prejudice," *First Things* 126 (October 2002): 23–24.

19. *The Persecution of the Catholic Church in the Third Reich* (Ft. Collins, CO: Roger McCaffrey Publishing, 1941), 321.

20. *Catechism*, 827.

21. Edward Hoffman, *The Right to Be Human: A Biography of Abraham Maslow* (Commack, NY: Four World's Press, 1988), 207.

22. Nancy Pearcy explains: "The notion that we need such a 'map' in the first place grows out of the biblical view of human nature. The Marxist may claim that human behavior is ultimately shaped by economic circumstances; the Freudian attributes everything to repressed sexual instincts; and the behavioral psychologist regards humans as stimulus-response mechanisms. But the Bible teaches that the overriding factor in the choices we make is our ultimate belief or religious commitment. Our lives are shaped by the 'god' we worship—whether the God of the Bible or some substitute deity." Pearcy, *Total Truth*, 23.

23. Henri Daniel-Rops, *The Church in the Dark Ages* (Garden City, NY: Image Books, 1962), vol. 2, 293.

24. Tom Hundley, "Tortured Priest's Tenacity Exposes Betrayal in Church," *Chicago Tribune* (February 26, 2007): 1.

Chapter 3

1. Cited in *Catechism of the Catholic Church* (Chicago: Loyola University Press, 1994), 826.

2. Ibid., 827.

3. Ibid.

4. Ibid., 1560, 894.

5. Ibid., 895.

6. Ibid., 888.

7. *Lumen gentium*, 25.

8. St. Augustine, *Sermon on Pastors* (Sermon 46, 9: CCL, 41), 535–36.

9. *Catechism*, 893.

10. St. Augustine, *Sermon*, 555–57.

11. *Catechism*, 1550.

12. Hans Urs von Balthasar, *Love Alone* (New York: Herder and Herder, 1989), 98–99.

13. Henri de Lubac, *Further Paradoxes* (Westminster, MD: Newman Press, 1958), 54.

14. Origen, *Contra Celsum*, in *The Ante-Nicene Fathers*, ed. Alexander Roberts and James Donaldson, vol. 4, B1, C3, ch. 58.

15. Ibid.

16. Ibid.

17. St. Augustine, *Sermon*, 529–30.

18. "Pope Relives Moment of His Election with Emotion" (Vatican City: Vatican Information Service, October 16, 2003), 1.

19. Ibid.

20. "John Paul II's Spiritual Testament" (Vatican City: Vatican Information Service, April 7, 2005), 1.

21. "Pope Relives Moment," 1.

22. Quoted in John Jay Hughes, "God's Mystery Surpasses All Our Learning." E-mail to associates, April 19, 2005, 2–3.

Chapter 4

1. William Marra, "We Overcame Their Faith: An Interview with Dr. William Coulson" *The Latin Mass: Chronicle of a Catholic Reform* (January–February, 1994): 12–17.

2. See Joyce Milton, *The Road to Malpsychia: Humanistic Psychology and Our Discontents* (San Francisco: Encounter

Books, 2002), chapter 5. Also William Marra, 'We Overcame Their Faith," Rosemary Curb and Nancy Manahan, eds., *Lesbian Nuns: Breaking Silence* (Tallahassee: Naiad Press, 1985); William R. Coulson, *Groups, Gimmicks and Instant Gurus* (New York: Harper and Row, 1972). See also for examples of indiscriminate openness: Don Clark, *Loving Someone Gay* (New York: New American Library, 1977) and Carl Rogers, *Carl Rogers on Person Power* (New York: Dell, 1977).

3. Marra, "We Overcame Their Faith," 13.

4. Ibid., 16.

5. Sally Feldman, "Why I'm Glad My Daughter Had Underage Sex" *The Humanist* 64 (November–December 2004): 9.

6. Judith Levine, *Harmful to Minors: The Perils of Protecting Children from Sex* (Minneapolis: University of Minnesota Press, 2002).

7. Lawrence S. Cunningham, "Thomas Merton Spiritual Master" (A Conversation at the Abbey of Gethsemani), sponsored by FADICA, 2002, 20.

8. Dorothy Day, *The Long Loneliness* (New York: Harper, 1952).

9. Ibid., 141.

10. Ibid., 139.

11. Ibid., 142.

12. Ibid., 149–50.

13. Ibid., 150.

14. Rosemary Haughton, "Marriage: An Old, New Fairy Tale," in *Marriage Among Christians,* ed. James Burtchaell (Notre Dame: Ave Maria Press, 1977), 132.

15. Ibid., 136.

16. Ibid., 140.

17. Ibid., 145.

18. Ibid., 146.

19. G. Ronald Murphy, SJ, *The Owl, The Raven, and the Dove: The Religious Meaning of Grimms' Magic Fairy Tales* (New York: Oxford University Press, 2000), 18.

Chapter 5

1. Anonymous, *The Persecution of the Catholic Church in the Third Reich* (Fort Collins, CO: Roger McCaffrey Publishing, 1941), 298–325.

2. Ibid., 305.

3. George Cardinal Mundelein, Archives of the Archdiocese of Chicago, Chancery Correspondence, Box 37, Folder 14, #136 entitled "Cardinal's Talk at Quarterly Conference, May 18, 1937," 1–5.

4. Anonymous, *Persecution*, 308.

5. Philip Jenkins, *The New Anti-Catholicism* (New York: Oxford University Press, 2003), 133.

6. Henri Daniel-Rops, *The Church in the Dark Ages* (Garden City, NY: Image Books, 1962), vol. 2, 293.

7. Ibid.

8. Ibid., 296.

9. Ibid., 296–97.

10. Ibid., 311.

Chapter 6

1. Osama bin Laden, *Fatwa*, February 1998.

2. Joseph Cardinal Ratzinger, *L'Osservatore Romano*, November 9, 1984.

3. Christopher A. Ferrara and Thomas E. Woods Jr., *The Great Façade: Vatican II and the Regime of Novelty in the Roman Catholic Church* (Wyoming, MN: The Remnant Press, 2002), 13.

4. Ibid.

5. Ibid., 14.

6. Ibid., 15.

7. Frank DeSiano, CSP, "Around the World of the Parish," *The Catholic World* (December 2006): 12.

8. "Debunking the Myths of Katrina," cover story in *Popular Mechanics* (March, 2006): 113–19.

9. John Berlau, *Eco-Freaks: Environmentalism Is Hazardous to Your Health* (Nashville: Thomas Nelson, 2006), 182.

10. Ibid., 183.

11. Ibid.

12. Ibid., 184.

Chapter 7

1. Martin Seligman, *Learned Helplessness* (New York: Oxford University Press, 1995). Seligman's work became the cutting edge of the new cognitive behavioral learning theory.

2. Ibid., 3.

3. Cited in Seligman, 64.

4. Albert Bandura, *Self-Efficacy* (New York: W. H. Freeman & Co., 1997), 58-59.

5. *The Dutch Catechism* (New York: Herder and Herder, 1967), 3.

Chapter 8

1. Cardinal Avery Dulles, "True and False Reform," *First Things* 135 (August–September 2003): 15.

2. Ibid.

3. "Church in the Modern World" in *Documents of the Vatican II*, 5b. To catch the spirit of this pastoral constitution and the confused, undifferentiated embrace of "modern science" read chapter 3 of Xavier Rynne's *The Fourth Session* (New York: Farrar, Straus and Giroux, 1965), 55–134.

4. Ibid., 54a.

5. Ibid., 62b.

6. Leone Algisi, *John XXIII* (London: Darton, Longman and Todd, 1963), 184–85.

7. John Tracey Ellis, "No Complacency," *America* (April 7, 1956): 24–25.

8. Dulles, "True and False Reform," 16.

9. Bernard Lonergan, *Collection* (London: Darton, Longman and Todd, 1967), 266–67.

10. St. Augustine, *The Confessions*, Book 10, 27.

11. Henri Daniel-Rops, *The Church in the Dark Ages* (Garden City, NY: Image, 1962), vol. 2, 78–79.

12. St. Augustine, *Sermon on Pastors* (Sermon 46, 9: CCL, 41) 535–36.

13. Daniel-Rops, *The Church in the Dark Ages*, vol. 2, 336–37.

14. St. Thomas Aquinas, *ST*, III, q. 8, a. 3, ad. 2.

15. Pope John XXIII, *Ad Petri cathedram*, June 29, 1959, 3.

16. *Lumen gentium*, 8.

17. Lonergan, *Collection* (New York: Herder and Herder, 1967), 259.

18. Bernard Lonergan, *Second Collection* (London: Darton, Longman and Todd, 1974), 163.

Chapter 9

1. Gene Edward Veith Jr., *Postmodern Times: A Christian Guide to Contemporary Thought and Culture* (Wheaton, IL: Crossway Books, 1994), 57, 192–97. See also Millard J. Erickson, *The Postmodern World* (Wheaton, IL: Rossway Books, 2002); David Harvey, *The Condition of Postmodernity* (Cambridge, MA: Basil Blackwell, 1989); Patricia Waugh, *Postmodernism: A Reader* (London: Edward Arnold, 1992); Steven Connor, *Postmodernist Culture* (Oxford: Basil Blackwell, 1989); Thomas C. Oden, *Two Worlds: Notes on the Death of Modernity in America and Russia* (Downers Grove, IL:

InterVarsity Press, 1992); David H. Hirsch, *The Deconstruction of Literature* (Hanover, NH: Brown University Press, 1991); Arthur Kroker, *Panic Encyclopedia: The Definitive Guide to the Postmodern Scene* (New York: St. Martin's Press, 1989). See also the philosophical writings of Jacques Derrida, Richard Rorty, Roland Barthes, Michel Foucault, and others.

2. Veith, *Postmodern Times,* 193–94.

3. Ibid., 195–97.

4. Ibid., 197–98.

5. Ibid., 29, 158–59.

6. Ibid., 202–3.

7. Tammy Bruce, *The New Thought Police* (New York: Three Rivers Press, 2001), 302.

8. Bruce, *New Thought Police,* 310.

9. Edward Rothstein, "Iconoclasm and Sacrilege" *New York Times* (June 9, 2001). Cited in Bruce, 304.

10. Terence Shimp, *Advertising, Promotion & Supplemental Aspects of Integrated Marketing Communications,* 6th ed. (Mason, OH: Thomson/Southwestern, 2003), 117–39.

11. Ibid., 121–27. See also Em Griffin, *A First Look at Communication Theory,* 4th ed. (New York: McGraw Hill, 2000), 190–201.

12. Anthony Pratkanis and Elliot Aronson, *Age of Propaganda: The Everyday Use and Abuse of Persuasion,* rev. ed. (New York: Henry Holt, 2001), 79–87.

13. Shimp, *Advertising,* 130.

14. Michael Warren, *Seeing Through the Media: A Religious View of Communications and Cultural Analysis* (Harrisburg, PA: Trinity Press, 1997), 182.

15. Bruce, *New Thought Police,* 2–3.

16. Marshall Kirk and Hunter Madsen, *After the Ball* (New York: Doubleday, 1989), 155.

17. Bruce, *New Thought Police,* 2–3.

18. Ibid., xvi.

19. Jean Danielou, SJ, *The Scandal of Truth* (London: The Catholic Book Club, 1962).

Epilogue

1. J. R. R. Tolkien, *The Fellowship of the Ring* (New York: Ballantine Books, 1969), 353.

A SELECTED
BIBLIOGRAPHY

Abbott, Walter, SJ. *The Documents of Vatican II*. New York: America Press, 1966.

Algisi, Leone. *John XXIII*. London: Darton, Longman, and Todd, 1963.

Anonymous, *The Persecution of the Catholic Church in the Third Reich*. Fort Collins, CO: Roger McCaffrey Publishing, 1941.

Augustine. *The Confessions*. New York: The Modern Library, 1949.

Augustine, *Retractationes*. Translated by Sister Mary Inez Bogan. Washington: Catholic University of America Press, 1968.

Augustine. *Sermon on Pastors*. CCL, 41.

Bandura, Albert. *Self-Efficacy*. New York: W. H. Freeman, 1997.

Berlau, John. *Eco-Freaks: Environmentalism Is Hazardous to Your Health*. Nashville: Thomas Nelson, 2006.

Bradshaw, John. *Bradshaw on The Family*. Deerfield Beach, FL: Health Communications, 1988.

Bruce, Tammy. *The New Thought Police.* New York: Three Rivers Press, 2001.

Canter, Lee and Marlene. *Assertive Discipline for Parents.* New York: Harper and Row, 1988.

Catechism of the Catholic Church. Chicago: Loyola University Press, 1994.

Catholic Eye, published by the National Committee of Catholic Laymen Inc., New York.

Clark, Don. *Loving Someone Gay.* New York: New American Library, 1977.

Connor, Steven. *Postmodernist Culture.* Oxford: Basil Blackwell, 1989.

Coulson, William R. *Groups, Gimmicks and Instant Gurus.* New York: Harper and Row, 1972.

Cox, Harvey. *The Secular City.* New York: Macmillan, 1965.

Cunningham, Lawrence S. "Thomas Merton Spiritual Master" (A Conversation at the Abbey of Gethsemani), sponsored by FADICA, 2002, 20.

Curb, Rosemary, and Nancy Manahan, eds. *Lesbian Nuns Breaking Silence.* Tallahassee: Naiad Press, 1985.

Daniel-Rops, Henri. *The Church in the Dark Ages.* Garden City, NY: Image Books, 1962.

Danielou, Jean, SJ. *The Scandal of Truth.* London: The Catholic Book Club, 1962.

Day, Dorothy. *The Long Loneliness.* New York: Harper, 1952.

"Debunking the Myths of Katrina." *Popular Mechanics* (March 2006): 113–19.

De Lubac, Henri. *Further Paradoxes.* Westminster, MD: Newman Press, 1958.

DeSiano, Frank, CSP. "Around The World of The Parish." *The Catholic World* (December 2006): 12.

Dreikurs, Rudolf. *The Challenge of Parenthood.* New York: Penguin, 1992.

Dulles, Cardinal Avery. "True and False Reform." *First Things* 135 (August–September 2003): 18.

The Dutch Catechism. New York: Herder and Herder, 1967.

Ellis, John Tracey. "No Complacency." *America* (April 7, 1956): 24–25.

Erickson, Millard J. *The Postmodern World.* Wheaton, IL: Crossway Books, 2002.

Fagan, Sean, SM. *Has Sin Changed?* Wilmington, DE: Michael Glazier, 1977.

Feldman, Sally. "Why I'm Glad My Daughter Had Underage Sex." *The Humanist* 64 (November–December 2004): 9.

Ferrara, Christopher A., and Thomas E. Woods Jr. *The Great Façade: Vatican II and the Regime of Novelty in the Roman Catholic Church.* Wyoming, MN: The Remnant Press, 2002.

Ginott, Haim. *Between Parent and Child.* New York: Macmillan, 1965.

Ginott, Haim. *Between Parent and Teenager.* New York: Macmillan, 1969.

Gordon, Thomas. *P.E.T. Parent Effectiveness Training.* New York: Penguin, 1970.

Gregory the Great. *Regula Pastoralis.* Translated by Henry David, SJ. Westminster, MD: The Newman Press, 1950.

Griffin, Em. *A First Look at Communication Theory.* 4th ed. New York: McGraw Hill, 2000.

Haag, Hebert. *Is Original Sin in Scripture?* Translated by Dorothy Thompson. New York: Sheed and Ward, 1969.

Harvey, David. *The Condition of Postmodernity.* Cambridge, MA: Basil Blackwell, 1989.

Haughton, Rosemary. "Marriage: An Old, New Fairy Tale." In *Marriage Among Christians,* edited by James Burtchaell, 130–46. Notre Dame: Ave Maria Press, 1977.

Hirsch, David H. *The Deconstruction of Literature.* Hanover, NH: Brown University Press, 1991.

Hoffman, Edward. *The Right to Be Human: A Biography of Abraham Maslow.* Commack, NY: Four World's Press, 1988.

Hundley, Tom. "Tortured Priest's Tenacity Exposes Betrayal in Church." *Chicago Tribune* (February 26, 2007): 1.

Jenkins, Philip. *The New Anti-Catholicism.* New York: Oxford University Press, 2003.

John XXIII. *Ad Petri cathedram* (June 29, 1959): 3.

A Selected Bibliography

Kehland, Medard, and Werner Loser. *The Von Balthasar Reader*. New York: Crossroads, 1982.

Kirk, Marshall, and Hunter Madsen. *After the Ball*. New York: Doubleday, 1989.

Kirschenbaum, Howard, and Valerie Land Henderson, eds. *Carl Rogers Reader*. Boston: Houghton Mifflin, 1989.

Kramer, Peter D. *Listening to Prozac: A Psychiatrist Explores Anti-Depressant Drugs and the Making of the Self*. New York: Viking, 1993.

Kroker, Arthur. *Panic Encyclopedia: The Definitive Guide to the Postmodern Scene*. New York: St. Martin's Press, 1989.

Lamb, Matthew, ed. *Creativity and Method: Essays in Honor of Bernard Lonergan*. Milwaukee: Marquette University Press, 1981.

Lasch, Christopher. *The Culture of Narcissism*. New York: Norton, 1978.

Leary, Timothy. *Flashbacks: A Personal and Cultural History of an Era*. New York: Putnam, 1981.

Levine, Judith. *Harmful to Minors: The Perils of Protecting Children from Sex*. Minneapolis: University of Minnesota Press, 2002.

Lonergan, Bernard. *Method in Theology*. New York: Herder and Herder, 1972.

Lonergan, Bernard. *Second Collection*. London: Darton, Longman and Todd, 1974.

Lowry, Richard J., ed. *The Journals of Abraham Maslow.* Monterey, CA: Brooks/Cole Publishing, 1984.

Mack, Dana. *The Assault on Parenthood.* New York: Simon & Schuster, 1997.

Marra, William. "We Overcame Their Faith: An Interview with Dr. William Coulson." *The Latin Mass: Chronicle of a Catholic Reform* (January–February 1994): 12–17.

Marzano, Robert J. *What Works in Schools.* Alexandria, VA: Association for Supervision and Curriculum Development, 2003.

Maslow, Abraham. *Toward a Psychology of Being.* New York: Van Nostrand Reinhold, 1968.

Menninger, Karl. *Whatever Became of Sin.* New York: Hawthorn Books, 1973.

Miller, Alice. *Drama of the Gifted Child: The Search for the True Self.* New York: Basic Books, 1994.

Miller, Alice. *For Your Own Good: Hidden Cruelty in Child-Rearing and the Roots of Violence.* New York: Noonday Press, 1983.

Milton, Joyce. *The Road To Malpsychia: Humanistic Psychology and Our Discontents.* San Francisco: Encounter Books, 2000.

Missildine, Whitney. *Your Inner Child of the Past.* New York: Simon & Schuster, 1993.

Morelli, Mark and Elizabeth, eds. *The Lonergan Reader.* Toronto: University of Toronto Press, 1997.

Mundelein, George Cardinal. "Chancery Correspondence." In *Archives of the Archdiocese of Chicago*. Box 37 (1937), Folder 14.

Murphy, G. Ronald, SJ. *The Owl, the Raven, and the Dove: The Religious Meaning of Grimms' Fairy Tales*. New York: Oxford University Press, 2000.

Oden, Thomas C. *Two Worlds: Notes on the Death of Modernity in America and Russia*. Downers Grove, IL: InterVarsity Press, 1992.

Origen, *Contra Celsum*. Alexander Roberts and James Donaldson., eds. *Ante-Nicene Fathers*. New York: Charles Scribner's Sons, 1925.

Pearcy, Nancy. *Total Truth: Liberating Christianity from Its Cultural Captivity*. Wheaton, IL: Crossway Books, 2004.

Pratkanis, Anthony, and Elliot Aronson. *The Age of Propaganda: The Everyday Use and Abuse of Persuasion*. Rev. edition. New York: Henry Holt, 2001.

Rogers, Carl. *Carl Rogers on Person Power*. New York: Dell, 1977.

Rogers, Carl. *On Becoming a Person*. Boston: Houghton Mifflin; 1961.

Schuller, Robert. *Self-Esteem: The New Reformation*. Nashville: Thomas Nelson, 1982.

Seligman, Martin. *Learned Helplessness*. New York: Oxford University Press, 1995.

Shimp, Terence. *Advertising, Promotion and Supplemental Aspects of Integrated Marketing Communications.* 6th ed. Mason, OH: Thompson/Southwestern, 2003.

Spock, Benjamin. *Baby and Child Care.* London: Star Books, 1983.

Sutterfield, Ragan. "No Easy Saint: Bonhoeffer and Just War." *Books and Culture* 11 (May–June 2005): 34.

Thomas Aquinas, *Summa Theologica.* Translated by Fathers of the English Dominican Province. New York: Benziger Brothers, 1947.

Tolkien, J. R. R. *The Fellowship of The Ring.* New York: Ballantine Books, 1969.

Veith Jr., Gene Edward. *Postmodern Times: A Christian Guide to Contemporary Thought and Culture.* Wheaton, IL: Crossway Books, 1994.

Vitz, Paul. *Faith of the Fatherless.* Dallas: Spence, 1999.

Vitz, Paul. "Support from Psychology for the Fatherhood of God." *Homiletic and Pastoral Review* 97 (February 1997): 7–19.

Warren, Michael. *Seeing Through the Media: A Religious View of Communications and Cultural Analysis.* Harrisburg, PA: Trinity Press, 1997.

Waugh, Patricia. *Postmodernism: A Reader.* London: Edward Arnold, 1992.

Woodward, Ken. "The Last Respectable Prejudice." *First Things* 126 (October 2002): 23–24.

A Selected Bibliography

Yankelovich, Daniel. *New Rules*. New York: Random House, 1981.

Zoch, Paul A. *Doomed to Fail*. Chicago: Ivan R. Dee Publisher, 2004.